"Theresa's new book is the ANTIDOTE to the mental virus that infects adults. With clear and persuasive prose she translates the mindfulness narrative of Jon Kabat-Zinn into practical ideas and advice that every CEO, Manager, Millennial, Gen X, and Baby Boomer will find massive value from. BRAVO for this masterwork!"

—DOUG HALL
Founder & Chairman of the Eureka! Ranch
Bestselling Author of *Driving Eureka!*
And *Jump Start Your Business Brain.*

Also by Theresa Puskar

8 Ways to Declutter Your Brain

THE GOOD MORNING MIND

9 ESSENTIAL MINDFULNESS HABITS FOR THE WORKPLACE

THERESA PUSKAR

MEDIA

MEDIA

Published 2020 by Gildan Media LLC
aka G&D Media
www.GandDmedia.com

Front cover design by David Rheinhardt of Pyrographx

Interior design by Meghan Day Healey of Story Horse, LLC

Library of Congress Cataloging-in-Publication Data is available upon request

ISBN: 978-1-7225-0267-6

10   9   8   7   6   5   4   3   2   1

Contents

Acknowledgments

Many people have helped to make this book possible. I am so grateful that you are in my life. I truly am blessed. I would like to offer my gratitude to:

My darling daughter, Bernadette, who brings such light and love into my life. Thank you for being you and especially for your design insights and suggestions.

My dear friend Susan Pluto, who, above and beyond providing me with huge emotional support, was also my second set of eyes. Your editing prowess is magical!

My longtime friend and constant rescuer, Jooley Johnson. Thank you for being my third set of eyes. I deeply appreciate your "intolerance" of poor grammar.

My thoughtful wasband (ex-husband), Paul, for your support and for your gift of my Wisconsin Dells time away from technology.

The wonderful staff at Oneness University in Chennai, India, and at the Dhamma Pakasa Vipassana Center in Pecatonica, Illinois.

Kent Palmer and the NaperLaunch team at Naperville Nichols Library, Naperville, Illinois, for their outstanding business program.

My three SCORE mentors, Chuck, Bruce, and Gerry. You gave outstanding advice, but more than that, you gave me hope when I was feeling down.

My biological and geographical families, both back home in Canada and here in Chicago.

Dan Strutzel, Gary Chappell, Vic Conant, and the Nightingale-Conant team. I am deeply grateful. The time I spent there set my life on a trajectory that has forever changed its course.

Tajuana Ross for being such a remarkable woman and outstanding coach.

Mindfulness can take you from a fear-based, egoic mentality into a place of deeper introspection, greater consciousness, and higher purpose. My intention in writing this book is to support you in creating a business environment that is committed to making more mindful choices. In doing so, you, your staff, and your business will no longer merely survive—you will thrive!

Prologue
The Early Morning Wake-up Call

It was predictable—like clockwork. Every morning at around 4:00 a.m. I would awaken from my sleep. Never sure why, and always lost in a fog of frustration and anger, I would stumble out of bed and head to the bathroom, or I would simply lie there, telling myself how tired I would be when my 7:00 a.m. alarm chimed. A storm of mixed emotions would ultimately form a massive tornado of anxiety within me.

I'm lost in thought about my never-ending to-do list. My body is tired, but my mind is racing; I can't turn it off. "This is going to screw up my day. This is not normal. Something is wrong with me. I'm going to get sick. Why does this keep on happening? Maybe I should just drink less water before bed. How many hours of sleep have I gotten? Oh, no. I'm going to want to pass out by noon tomorrow if I don't get enough sleep. Dang, I've got to go back to sleep. Shoot—I forgot to water the garden. Need to do that before heading to work. Oh, and then I've got to pay my credit card bill . . . if I don't get that in by Tuesday, I'll have to pay a late fee. And speaking of late, why the heck does the neighbor's dog make such a racket so late at night? Boy, that really ticks me off! Back to my to-do list. Groceries—can't forget to buy milk. Man, I just can't shut this crazy mind down. How the heck am I ever going to get back to sleep? Maybe if I listen to the radio, it'll quiet my mind. Hmmm, not working. Maybe if I . . . what if I . . . Grrrrr!"

Sound familiar? Your body is tired, and it is clearly telling you so, but your mind is racing a mile a minute. No matter how hard you try, you just can't shut it down.

Perhaps You Experience the Opposite

Perhaps you are at the opposite end of the spectrum, where you experience the good night mind. You are wide awake and raring to go until late in the night (or often early the next morning). It may be difficult to turn your mind off in order to get to sleep. However, once you are asleep, you are like a lead weight. In the morning, sixteen alarms go off and you hear none of them. When you finally awaken, you are late for work. You feel exhausted, miserable, and uninterested in the day ahead.

Whether you consider yourself to be a morning or a night person, this syndrome doesn't just happen during our sleep cycles. Whenever you find yourself trapped in a web of negative or worrisome thoughts that you can't turn off, you are suffering. Often this crazy brain chatter happens at the most inopportune times—when you are stressed by a tight deadline and you are trying to finish a work project, when you are supposed to be compassionately listening to a friend in need, or when you simply have a moment to yourself and want to find a bit of peace and quiet. It is a menace. It is constant and seemingly uncontrollable.

The Good Morning Mind Shift

For several years, I found myself struggling with this cycle of incessant mind chatter. It kept me awake and anxious until one morning when I finally decided to acquiesce. I gave up, and instead of fighting the crazy monkey mind that would not stop chattering, I set an intention to do something different. I lay in bed and took a couple of deep, calming breaths. I thought, "I'm going to surrender. I am going to open my mind and heart right now and see where it takes me." So I did, and with every inhale, I said the word "yes" to myself. With every exhale, I imagined a day ahead that would be easy, effortless, and filled with joy. I imagined myself being highly productive, enjoying what I was doing, and connecting with colleagues. I saw myself exercising, and my mouth watered as I imagined eating healthy, scrumptious meals. I saw myself having a delightfully delicious day. I shifted from a place of restlessness and resistance to a place of welcome. In doing so I discovered my Good Morning Mind.

As I practiced this technique, I soon found myself falling back to sleep. I would subsequently wake up feeling vitalized, refreshed, and enthusiastic about the day ahead.

Whether you find yourself in a similar situation or are unable to function because you always feel sleep-deprived, you can resolve it, not necessarily by shifting your sleep habits, but by changing your waking awareness and intentions.

Only the Beginning

This is not the end of the story. In fact, it's really where it begins. Saying an unqualified "yes" became a practice that I wanted to expand throughout all aspects of my life. Little did I know that it would take me on a one-month adventure to India and back again. It also took me to a silent, ten-day *vipassana* retreat. There I meditated for twelve hours each day and explored the recesses of my mind. It provided me with insights that allowed me to see the truth behind my nightly disturbances. I learned that they extended far beyond nighttime into just about every area of my life.

My Good Morning Mind commitment led me on a journey towards deepening my relationship with myself. The more I explored, the more I realized that I was not who I thought that I was. I was lying to myself and to my Creator. I was manipulating myself and others in ways of which I was completely unaware. I was reactive more than proactive. I was believing I was a victim, both personally and in my career.

I also discovered that I was filled with self-contempt and my mind was fixed in a whirlwind of self-condemnation. I realized that I was labeling myself as the thoughts that I thought and the feelings that I felt. Sometimes I was the angry woman. Other times I was the dutiful and unappreciated employee, the shamed daughter, or the guilty and defective mother. As I continued to root the "yes" practices and intentions into my daily routine, the more I was led to the extraordinary world of deep self-discovery.

What the Good Morning Mind Can Experience

When I was in my early twenties, I realized that my deepest soul's calling was to fall fully and madly in love with myself, and in doing so, to support others in falling in love with themselves. From an early age, I believed that at my center I was ugly and dark. I judged the heck out of myself and consequently those around me. The deeper I criticized myself, the more I hated myself, and the more I judged others. It became a growing cycle of contempt.

Once I started integrating the Good Morning Mind intentions and practices into my life, incremental shifts started to happen. Starting my day with an open-hearted "yes" gradually shifted my fear-based, self-loathing perceptions to more accepting and loving ones. Many aspects of my life began to change.

The angry, reactive pit in my stomach started to loosen. Not only was I able to see the part I played in the dramas of my life, but I was also able to feel much greater compassion towards myself and others. The heaviness of guilt and regret started to lift.

My relationship with myself became more authentic. I was able to look at the parts of myself that I was reluctant to see. As I did, layers and layers of who I thought I was were peeled away. I was left to discover who I really was beyond my human failings and foibles.

The world started opening up for me. Opportunities for travel, creative expressions, financial support, and career moves that were in alignment with my soul's message would magically and delightfully appear. Synchronistic connections and prospects would unfold in response to the intentions I created. The blocks that were once in the way were lifted, and I was in sync with the flow of our benevolent and supportive universe.

As I became more present, my relationships flourished. I was able to be more of an active listener and connect with others on a deeper level. Inauthentic relationships revealed themselves to me, and I was able to put more time and energy into co-creative relationships that increased my energy and raised my consciousness.

I was able to get very clear about who I am and what I want. I felt less encumbered by the shaming "should" voice within me and more energized by the "yes" voice that had my best interest at heart. I learned to say a gentle, open-hearted "no" to others when a commitment did not energetically feed me. In doing so, I was able to maintain my dignity and self-love while honoring my own needs.

Now I experience a great deal more peace in my life. I am better able to choose my actions from a place of thoughtful proactivity over knee-jerk reactivity. I am less explosive and more level-headed. I can now grow calm and quiet in five minutes. That's all it takes.

I feel the deepest appreciation for my life, to the point of experiencing causeless joy. At times my heart is overwhelmed with awe and gratitude to the point of uncontrollable laughter and tears. The more I am able to integrate the Good Morning Mind practices into my work life, the less I experience it as work. It is joyful creativity in action!

There is so much that I am excited to share with you in the pages ahead. What does it take to implement these habits into your work life? Strong, focused intentions, a deep commitment to inner integrity, and a willingness to say an emphatic "yes" to yourself!

Introduction

You most likely picked up this book because you need to find a better, more solid, and more productive way to function. Whether you are a leader in the corporate world, a burgeoning entrepreneur, or a staff member within a business large or small, I created this book for you. To simplify things, I refer to situations from the perspective of the business manager. However, the habits, theories, practices, and examples speak to everyone in the working population, whatever your role might be.

While technology has taken us to new heights, it has also been the demise of many formerly viable businesses. These days you have to have a solid foundation while being flexible enough to shift how you do business instantaneously when necessary. To develop the strength to maintain, alter, or even restructure your business when required, it must be based on incredibly strong roots. "Outings" of businesses or individuals who lacked integrity and were rooted in lies have been growing. The world no longer has patience for unyielding greed, flagrant irresponsibility, or rigid doctrine.

When your business interactions are rooted in a foundation of integrity, creativity, and diversity, like a tree whose roots run deep, it can bend in the wake of pending storms. Integrating mindfulness practices and raising the consciousness within your business is the right thing to do. It also strengthens its energetic imprint on the earth, bolstering the planet's chances for survival.

What Is a Good Morning Mind?

The Good Morning Mind sets your energy for the day. It starts in the direction of delightful, delicious expectation and expands upon that energetic intention throughout your day and into the rest of your life. It is a reprogramming of your attitude from a "no" or "not today" intention to an enthusiastic "yes, yes, yes" response to your life. There will always be bumps in the road, but experiencing them from a "yes" mindset will take you from seeing yourself as a helpless victim to knowing that you are a powerful victor. With the Good Morning Mind, you are integrating your heart into the equation. Although you can't change difficult people or situations, you *can* change the way you perceive them. Therein lies your freedom.

I look forward to taking you on a journey of discovery that goes beyond what your mind can currently comprehend. I have broken down the essential requirements for a successful business into nine habits. When you cultivate the Good Morning Mind and integrate the behaviors and practices that I outline for you, your business relationships can flourish, and your business can soar to new heights. The nine habits spell out the acronym BE PRESENT. At the core of each habit is a solid commitment to living in the present moment. This takes discipline, courage, and a willingness to explore all of yourself—both what you embrace as good and what you condemn as harmful.

What Exactly Is Mindfulness?

Mindfulness has become a real buzzword, especially in the world of business. But what exactly is it? I find the word to be a bit of a dichotomy. If the act of mindfulness is the act of quieting the mind, then why do we call it mind*full*ness? Isn't it the opposite?

I suggest that the mind is always full. Our challenge (or opportunity) is to get comfortable with its fullness; in time, our relationship with it will shift. We will be able to get to a place of quieting even in spite of it.

In a nutshell, mindfulness meditation is a mental practice that involves focusing your mind on your experiences (bodily sensations, thoughts, or feelings) as they arise in the present moment. Thoughts pass through the mind constantly. They are often repetitive, focusing on regrets about the past or issues that could arise in the future. They are very often fear-based. Getting lost in yesterday and tomorrow, we miss out on experiencing life in the present moment. As we practice mindfulness, which is simply sitting quietly and observing our thoughts, we start to cultivate the witness-self. This self is the watcher of the thoughts. In the same way that you sit and watch a movie, your witness-self is able to watch your thoughts as they arise. It sees them come and go as if they were clouds passing through your mind.

Cultivating Curiosity

As your witness-self develops, you become more and more curious. You are able to watch the drama around you unfold as you are living it. As you play your role in the performance of your life, another part of you is able to detach and neutrally observe it. This neutrality comes from your commitment to non-judgment. It requires setting an intention to feel compassion first and foremost for yourself. Once you experience this compassion, you will naturally find yourself feeling it towards others. You will experience firsthand the realization that your external harshness and judgments are rooted in your own self-criticism. Once you commit to self-love, life starts to fall into place.

Ultimately, as you develop your wise observer self, you start to have a dialogue with it. You are able to choose differently, to step away from the drama. Although currently you may not find comfort in stillness, there will likely come a time when you will welcome it. You will start to experience how good it feels simply to sit in silent observation. You can feel the life force coursing through your veins. There is a freedom, a liberation, in simply sitting, observing, and being totally present.

An Exercise in Mindfulness

Before you begin, I encourage you to turn off your phone and create an environment in which you will not be disturbed. Find a quiet, relaxing place to sit with your spine straight and your back erect. I usually have pillows to support my back, and I cover myself with a couple of comfortable blankets. If you wish, you can set a timer. If you have not practiced meditation in the past, you may find that you only want to sit for five minutes. If you find you can only last two minutes, so be it. The more you practice meditating, the more you will be able to increase the duration. Above all else, be sure not to judge yourself. The fact that you are making this commitment is enough.

Now close your eyes and simply observe your breath. Feel the cool air just below your nostrils as you breathe in. Feel the warm air that is exiting your nostril on each exhalation. Continue doing this, simply observing. You will likely find that thoughts enter into your mind. When you notice that you have strayed from observing your breath, simply note it: "Oh, I was just thinking about . . ." and then go back to observing your breath.

Once you feel ready to leave the meditation, take a moment to repeat the word "yes" to yourself. As you do so, imagine a white light filling your heart. See your heart opening, and see that light expanding to fill each cell of your body. Then see yourself having an awesome day ahead, as if you are experiencing it in the present moment (like a movie). Imagine yourself feeling joyful and laughing, enjoying your work or play, and having wonderful connections with your coworkers, friends, and family. Imagine experiencing all that you desire easily and effortlessly manifesting in the day ahead. If you are to do this each morning when you awaken, you will probably find that you are energetically clearing pathways towards a better day.

In the evenings, before going to sleep, I encourage you to do the same. This time, during the "yes" mantra, observe the day you just had in your mind's eye. Reflect on the experiences and all that you are grateful for. Re-experience everything that brought you pleasure. It could be as simple as tasting a succulent orange or smelling a freshly brewed cup of coffee. You can feel grateful for your functioning umbrella or for the fact that your car got you to work on time. Your appreciations don't have to be big, but be sure to seek out things that you are truly grateful for. Doing this exercise before going to sleep puts you in an energetically positive space to support a good night's sleep.

You may not like sitting in stillness. In fact, you may have resisted doing this short meditation. That's just fine. Don't give up. (For years, I resisted, and I did not enjoy meditating.) I encourage you to keep reading and trying, even if only for a couple of minutes each day. The discomfort and frustration that you may feel will be well worth it in the end. As we progress through the book, I will provide you with additional mindfulness tools and techniques to assist you in further cultivating your meditative mindset.

Realizing Resistance

The first step in cultivating the Good Morning Mind is to see your resistance for what it is. I spent over twenty years as a writer and producer in the self-empowerment world. In 1999, I got a job at Nightingale-Conant Corporation, which at the time was the world's largest publisher of motivational audiobooks. I was surrounded by mindfulness experts and was privileged to work with outstanding teachers like Jon Kabat-Zinn, Dr. David Hawkins, and Gregg Braden. They had all mastered the art of mindfulness and constantly reminded me of its benefits. I knew that sitting in stillness would bring me a greater sense of calm, nonreactivity, and clarity. But for over fifteen years, I could not bring myself to do so. My mind fought it every step of the way.

However, as I started the "yes" intention, allowing and anticipating good things to come my way, the opportunity to practice mindfulness arose. It started in 2013, when I headed to the Oneness University in Chennai, India. They offered a one-month introspective process known as the Deepening. I heard about it years prior when I produced a couple of audiobooks with metaphysical teacher and healer Ron Roth. He had been to India and had visited the founder of Oneness University, Shri Amma Bhagavan. He was so altered by his experience there that he sent his entire staff to the program and constantly spoke of Bhagavan's powerful work. The desire to attend someday had been planted in my brain, and for years I kept bumping into people who had attended. They attested to the fact that it was the most transformational experience they ever had. I knew that one day I would experience it myself.

When that day came, I was both enthusiastic and cautious. Unlike some of my friends, I never had a burning desire to visit India. But because I had heard so much about this program, I welcomed the experience. On the third day of the retreat, we were instructed to meditate in the center's massive and exquisite temple. It was difficult to close my eyes. Just taking in the physical beauty and energetic magnificence of this extraordinary portal was overwhelming. And let's face it: I was terrible at sitting in stillness. Whenever I tried to meditate, I'd last no more than five minutes before jumping up to complete a task that popped into my head. Sound familiar?

An Introduction to Causeless Joy

The first time I attempted to meditate at the temple, I heard a loud, obnoxious cackling sound. It grew louder, and then it started coming from multiple sources. I opened my eyes only to see that the sound was coming from some of the meditators. They were laughing. They sounded like a bunch of rabid monkeys (not that

I've ever heard rabid monkeys, and I hope I never do!). As I sat unable to focus on quieting my mind, a volcano of anger began to build inside of me. Just as it was ready to erupt, a clear, commanding voice in my head spoke, "Girlfriend, that so-called 'annoyance' is an outer reflection of your monkey mind. Get over it!" I laughed to myself at the clarity and perfection of that message. It was true. As I eased into the message, I was able to take myself and my inability to concentrate much less seriously. To my amazement, I later learned that those cackling meditators were experiencing bliss—causeless joy. I had no idea that joy could be so annoying! I'll be sharing a great deal more about causeless joy in the pages that follow. Suffice it to say that you can begin to experience this benefit once you implement mindfulness and the nine habits of the Good Morning Mind.

The Door Opens

The seed of experiencing mindfulness that was planted in India was cultivated in an even more profound way a year later at the Dhamma Pakasa Vipassana Meditation Center in Pecatonica, Illinois. Soon after returning from India, I was instructed by a dear friend and metaphysical teacher, Bharat Kalra, to attend the silent ten-day vipassana retreat. Despite all of the emotional and spiritual work that I had done in India and for decades prior, he informed me that my energy centers were imbalanced and that mindfulness practices would help to remedy the situation.

Taking his advice, I attended the retreat. India was a piece of cake compared to this. People ask, "How could you remain in silence for ten days?" The silence was easy; sitting and observing my crazy brain and all of its tricks, traps, and repetitive spin cycles for twelve hours a day was my greatest challenge. After spending ten full days in this regimen, spending one hour a day is easy. It's all relative!

One Moment, Many Perspectives

To clarify how mindfulness functions, here is an example of the workings of your mind as you integrate it into your daily routine. Recently I recorded the audio version of my previous book, *8 Ways to Declutter Your Brain*. Prior to cultivating mindfulness, I would have been reading the manuscript and simply reacting to input from my engineers. My mind would have wandered into some fear of what might come to pass tomorrow or regrets about what happened yesterday. While I would have completed the task, I would rarely have actually been present and fully committed to the moment. But after practicing mindfulness for several years, I was able to be more present.

Having cultivated the witness-self, I was also experiencing the moment from a variety of personae. I was relating to the message on the manuscript in front of me as the reader of my material. At the same time, I was wearing my producer hat and editing the performance (for example, "I'm speeding up here, and I need to repeat the last two sentences and slow down"). I was also wearing my observer hat as I watched the interplay between my performer and producer selves. The witness-self exists in each moment and sees the whole picture from a wider lens of knowingness.

To be clear, I wasn't always in the present moment during the two eight-hour days of recording. Even with the cultivation of mindfulness, our consciousness tends to move in and out of the present. Few can sustain it until they reach the state of enlightenment.

There were, however, key moments when I was in the zone. I was so present and tuned into the message that I made no errors and it flowed effortlessly. The sentiments I expressed were heartfelt and deep. I anticipate that those segments will prove to be the most powerful.

Imagine being able to cultivate a work environment in which your staff frequently experiences being in the zone. Creativity and innovation would flourish, and a sense of greater harmony would prevail.

The Invisible Energy of Presence

Ultimately, I believe that mindfulness enabled me to create a product that was much more focused and dynamic. When you are totally committed to the present moment, there is an invisible energy that draws others to you. This happens because of your heightened awareness. For example, when I teach preschool children, when I am present with them, they feel it. When they speak, I hear them and respond accordingly. When sadness arises in one of them, I am more connected and immediately respond. I am able to note it and address it so that the child feels seen, heard, and loved. Ultimately, I believe that on the playground of life, whether we are aged three or 103, each of us wants to be seen and understood. When we are, we feel a sense of safety and calm.

At the workplace, when you cultivate mindfulness and present-moment awareness in your organization, there is a greater sense of calm, safety, and well-being among your staff. The energy of the environment shifts from fear-based reactivity to love-based proactivity.

Cultivating the witness-self ultimately provides you with a more balanced and objective perspective on situations as they arise. At times, it almost feels as if you are watching the movie of your life unfold in slow motion. You are able to adjust and step away from reactive knee-jerk choices into more conscious ones.

I hope you are beginning to see how mindfulness and the cultivation of the witness-self can hugely affect your experiences in the workplace. Imagine an entire staff, all of whom have cultivated the witness-self and are committed to raising their own consciousness. Calmness would prevail, along with a sense of deep purpose and altruism that is not forced, but natural and organic, as each employee grows in compassion and self-awareness.

Beyond Meditation: Introspection

While many business mindfulness programs focus on meditation and calming techniques, the mindfulness that I am speaking of here goes a step further. It's about cultivating a culture of deep inner integrity and introspection. It is about evolving yourself and your business into a completely new paradigm. It's about doing the emotional work along with mindfulness practices. If we practice meditation and present-moment awareness, but we are not willing to look at the ways in which we trick ourselves and those around us, we will only reach a certain point in our evolution.

This book is about making a massive shift toward self-accountability and having the courage to look within ourselves. It is about making a choice to own our part in the dramas of our lives and to stop claiming to be victims of external circumstances. To get to this state, you have to be willing to do the challenging inner inventory. The awesome thing is that the more you do, the more you will attract others to you who are also committed to their own personal growth.

You Are Not Your Thoughts

As time passed, and the more I integrated my mindfulness practices into my personal growth regimen, the more I was able to cultivate the neutral witness-self. I could view the role I was playing in the drama of my life from an impersonal stance. Then one day, my teacher in India shared a lesson: "You are not your thoughts. Just as the air you breathe is part of the atmosphere, the thoughts you think are part of the thoughtmosphere."

How life-altering that statement was! I realized that I had labeled myself based on the feelings that I had and the thoughts that ran through my mind. I believed that I was the anger that I felt; I was the shame that welled up inside me. I believed I personified every unkind thought that I had about myself and others. Once I realized that I was more than those thoughts or feelings, I truly felt liberated.

Who Are You?

What if, after being on this earth for so many years, you realized that you are not who you think you are? You are not the body you carry or the mind that reacts. You are not the personality who has disdain for some and deep love for others. In fact, you are not even the thinker. It is the machine called the mind that is thinking and producing the illusion of a thinker. You are the witness. You are the watcher whose task it is to build a greater sense of compassion and understanding for yourself and others. Your job is to observe the triggers in your life as they occur, then feel into the emotions that arise in response, resisting nothing. Simply feel into them. Then watch as the emotions guide you on your journey towards deeper love and understanding.

Watch Stress Melt Away

Much of the stress you experience comes from your attempts to resist your feelings as they arise. You often want to repress them and stuff them inside. As the witness-self becomes more aware, you are able to view situations and your responses to them with more compassion and neutrality. Instantaneous shifts in consciousness, though possible, are rare. As I have mentioned, there were several stages in this journey that took me to the place where I experience myself differently.

I look forward to taking you through a myriad of steps that propel you out of misguided self-perceptions and into the Good Morning mindset. Cultivating a Good Morning Mind and bringing it to your business will exponentially increase productivity, relationships, well-being, and your bottom line. The workplace will no longer be a drab place that you have to tolerate for forty hours a week so that you can earn a paycheck in the hopes that someday you'll be happy. It can be the place that fosters personal growth, builds solid relationships, and nurtures innovation that is beyond anything you could ever imagine.

A Leap of Faith

To fully receive the gifts that the Good Morning Mind offers, you have to be willing to open your mind and heart and take a leap of faith. Some of the stories I share will be a stretch for your logical, skeptical mind, but I can assure you that they are true. And while your monkey mind may wish to dismiss the practices I will offer, I strongly encourage you to give them a try. They worked for me and for many of the people I mention in these pages.

While I look forward to taking you with me on a journey of discovery that goes beyond what your mind can currently comprehend, it is my intention to meet you where you are on your consciousness-raising journey. Each habit chapter will be structured as follows:

1. At the beginning, I will provide you with a profile or emotional inventory survey to help you determine where you are compared to where you would like to be. Doing so provides you with greater clarity to support you in your initiatives.

2. Each habit chapter will include a trigger anecdote: a story about a disturbance in the workplace that can be remedied through Good Morning Mind insights and practices.

3. After each trigger situation, I will provide three response scenarios based on one's level of consciousness or emotional positions: the perspective of the mind (reactive, victim, ego, resistant); the wisdom of the heart (trusting, proactive, self-accountable, open, and possessing inner integrity); and the awakened perspective of the witness-self (preactive, surrendered, responding in absolute faith, and committed to organic altruism). To explain each of the three states:

   • When you respond to any situation with the voice of the mind, you tend to be highly reactive. By "mind" here I mean the fight-or-flight, reptilian part of the brain. When you respond from this part of your psyche, you are defensive, reactive, and acting from a place of fear. To be clear, I am not maligning the reptilian brain. It is valuable and necessary for functioning, but it is overused. Centuries ago, when you were living out in the wild, you needed it to survive. Originally it was meant to be fired up when, say, we were being chased by a lion. This is no longer the case. Nonetheless, with all of the stressors we are trying to overcome in present society, many of us are frequently caught in the reptilian brain's fight-or-flight stance. For many of us, our adrenals are overworked because we remain in this defensive stance throughout a good part of the day. We are burnt out because we don't feel safe. We don't feel heard or understood. We are looking for solace outside of ourselves, but everyone else is so lost in their own fears that they cannot be present for us.

In fact, nobody could be present in a way that would calm our fears. You need to develop an internal messaging system that does this for you. Cultivating the internal nurturer (the Good Morning Mind) will calm the reptilian brain. Until that time, when responding from the reptilian brain, you are led by your ego. You often feel angry and victimized. You see yourself as innocent and blame the other for your demise. You consciously or unconsciously put up an energetic wall of protection, keeping your heart and mind closed. An adversarial environment is created, and tension builds in the workplace.

- When you respond from your heart, you are more contemplative, because you have started to cultivate the witness-self. You are dissociating yourself from the reptilian brain. You can watch the drama unfold, and in doing so, you have greater insight into your responsibilities in the interplay. Although your ego may be reacting to a degree, you are able to step back and witness its dance in a more neutral and non-judgmental way. You are less reactive and more proactive. You hold yourself in higher esteem, and as a result you are willing to be accountable for the roles you play in your dramas. You trust that all will be resolved. You find a compromise, or you are willing to agree to disagree.

- When you have cultivated an awakened state in yourself, you respond from the guidance of your witness-self. You have reached a state of complete surrender. You are not attached to being right. You have absolute faith that all will work out for the highest good of all involved. You have developed a sense of altruism, not from a place of "I should . . ." but from an organic understanding. In fact, you often act from a place of what I will call *preactivity*. In your present-moment awareness, you are able to hear that still voice of guidance from within, so much so that you can often anticipate an issue before it manifests. While this may sound absurd, we know how animals possess a sixth sense. Sometimes dogs sense their owners' cancer and nudge at the area in which it is sitting in the body until the owner calls the doctor to investigate. We see this trait in many animals who can smell danger and run to safety before they are pounced on by a hungry tiger. In this state, you know that you are the witness, not the individual experiencing the drama. You experience yourself as a part of a greater field of consciousness; you are focused and committed to seeing the innocence in all. This does not mean that you are passive. In fact, in many cases you are more responsive, but your choices come from a place of greater clarity and knowing.

To be clear, I am not fully awakened. While I have glimpses of that state, at this time I do not embody it completely. But throughout my career, I have been privileged to work with awakened, enlightened masters. I can only speak of this state through the knowledge and insights that they have shared with me. I believe that referring to this state will inspire the desire to attain it.

Reviewing responses to trigger scenarios from these three tiers of consciousness will serve as a barometer for your current state. It will provide you with a sense of where you have come from, where you currently are, and where you could potentially be as you continue along your path of personal growth, mindfulness, and self-awareness.

4. Each habit section will end with Innovative Implementation Ideas. These are suggestions on how you might implement the habit into the workplace in a fun and creative way.

5. The initials of the names of the habits outlined in this book spell the statement BE PRESENT. As you journey through this book, your efforts to be present with all that transpires in your life lie at the core of transforming you and your business. Being present is at the heart of mindfulness. It is responsible for integrating calm, work-life balance, and all the other benefits that this system has to offer.

What It Means to Be Present

When I say that being present is at the core of each of the nine habits, what do I mean? Once we commit to being conscious, we start to see how much we live in a place of fear. In fact, I believe that most us suffer because we see the world around us through the eyes of fear rather than love. Our minds are constantly spinning on a treadmill of repetitive thoughts, most of which dwell on angst, shame, and resentment about the past, or in fear, anxiety, and anticipation about the future. If we were able to let go of past grievances and not anticipate future potential pain, we could be fully present in each moment.

When you can witness your life unfold in the present, you can recontextualize the mundane as you start to see the miracles in every moment. You are able to be connected with others on a much deeper level—you see them, and they see you—because you are not lost in your thoughts. You will experience more and more synchronicities as you shift from fear-based thinking to being present as an eager witness to the unfolding of your life.

Choosing the Right Mindset

Later I will show you how to integrate the nine essential habits into your business. To start, here is a general overview of the state of consciousness you want to be in so that you are open and receptive to shifting into the Good Morning Mind.

It starts with being *intentional*. While most of us begin our day willy-nilly, studies have shown that when we start the day setting specific intentions, we are more likely to attract what we set our minds to. In other words, there is a law of attraction, and intention is the key that unlocks the door from mere thought to actual manifestation.

Countless studies support this theory. One of my favorites is the water experiments of Japanese scientist Dr. Masaru Emoto. He would record images of polluted water crystals, then he would expose the water to a variety of stimuli. In one experiment, he had monks chant over a polluted pond for an extended period of time. The "before" images of the water were dark, murky, and disorganized. However, after being exposed to the energy that came from the focused chants of the monks, the water crystals became clear and organized and were rearranged into beautiful geometric shapes.

Whether you believe in the power of intention or not, you can experience it for yourself. Take a moment and think about a lemon. Pay attention to your body and any physical reactions that you experience when contemplating the lemon. You usually notice that your mouth begins to water, and you salivate as you consider its sourness.

Similarly, when you set your sights on what you enjoy and focus on experiencing gratitude, you feel more joy. You feel energized and better than you would have had you been focusing your attention on a negative or traumatic experience. As you feel good, your vitality increases, and you have additional momentum toward experiencing more of what you desire in your life. When your energy is higher, you are more likely to be productive, optimistic, calmer, creative, harmonious, and focused. Starting your day in the Good Morning way can set you on a path towards manifesting more positive and proactive experiences in your life.

Setting your intentions towards *starting your day in a receptive mode* gets your energetic engine running with clean fuel. Before taking any action in your day, lie in bed and say a definitive "yes." Whenever you feel your heart close throughout your day, stop and take a moment to breathe into your heart, while repeating "yes." See your heart opening. I find that doing this reprograms the mind from fear to trust. From this open-hearted place, more grounded and balanced decisions are made.

As you set your clear and earnest intentions and commit to being in a state of complete receptivity, the wisdom of the nine essential habits will ignite a natural appreciation within you. Ultimately, as your heart and mind expand, you will experience more intoxicating joy in your life and in your business.

Mindfulness Matrix Profile

Before you delve into learning the nine habits and how to integrate them into your business, it would be helpful for you to gain insights on the extent to which you already incorporate mindfulness into it. You may be consciously integrating mindfulness or doing so without even being aware of it. Either way, clarity will provide you with a matrix upon which you can get a sense of where you are compared to where you would like to be. For each of the questions below, choose the number that most closely aligns with your current views, mindset or situation (1 being "not at all" and 10 being "a great deal").

1. Do you meet deadlines and deliver without chaos, stress, or confusion?

1 — 2 — 3 — 4 — 5 — 6 — 7 — 8 — 9 — 10

2. Does your staff remain with your business for long durations?

1 — 2 — 3 — 4 — 5 — 6 — 7 — 8 — 9 — 10

3. Does your workplace flow with a sense of ease, joy, and laughter?

1 — 2 — 3 — 4 — 5 — 6 — 7 — 8 — 9 — 10

4. Are conflicts resolved quickly, without creating long-term resentment?

1 — 2 — 3 — 4 — 5 — 6 — 7 — 8 — 9 — 10

5. Does your staff feel respected, heard, trusted, and appreciated?

1 — 2 — 3 — 4 — 5 — 6 — 7 — 8 — 9 — 10

6. Do you encourage community over competitiveness among your staff?

1 — 2 — 3 — 4 — 5 — 6 — 7 — 8 — 9 — 10

7. Do you encourage self-care as a priority among your staff?

1 — 2 — 3 — 4 — 5 — 6 — 7 — 8 — 9 — 10

8. Do you share your successes with your staff?

1 — 2 — 3 — 4 — 5 — 6 — 7 — 8 — 9 — 10

9. Do your staff, clients, and partners feel they can be open and honest with you?

1 — 2 — 3 — 4 — 5 — 6 — 7 — 8 — 9 — 10

10. Do you frequently express gratitude towards your staff, partners, and clients?

1 — 2 — 3 — 4 — 5 — 6 — 7 — 8 — 9 — 10

If you scored between 76 and 100, you run a very evolved, productive, and supportive business. In general, you tend to your staff and you have created an environment that encourages community, connection, self-assertiveness, pride, and an element of fun. Following the practices outlined in this book can bring you less stress and even greater success!

If you scored between 51 and 75, you are well on your way to creating a mindful work environment. Understanding and implementing the Good Morning Mind insights and practices can further enhance your workplace, encouraging true authenticity, integrity, and honesty. As you integrate mindfulness into your business, you can expect greater ease, calm, and harmony.

If you scored between 26 and 50, while you have some mindfulness in your business, it could use a great deal more. Focus on the tools and practices in this book in order to move your business into a greater sense of ease, well-being, productivity, and proficiency. You will see changes, especially among your staff and in the way that they engage with you and one another.

If you scored between 10 and 25, your business requires a great deal more mindfulness. Kudos to you for having the foresight and drive to pick up this book! The good news is that you are willing to be truthful and introspective in completing this profile. With integrity and honesty at your core, when you follow these lessons with the same commitment, you can experience tremendous shifts for the better.

The BE PRESENT Business Model

HABIT		DESCRIPTION
Habit 1	**B**	**BUILD** a solid foundation based on honor and integrity: the micro reflects the macro. Transparency is the ideal and must be rooted in honor and honesty, both among staff members and within the organization as a whole.
Habit 2	**E**	**EMBOLDEN** your staff. Encourage self-accountability, pride, and ownership. Incentivizing them from a place of internal empowerment energizes them, because they will feel seen, heard, and appreciated.
Habit 3	**P**	**PLACATE** fear. Expel constrictive mindsets, build security, and ignite creative genius. Doing so will keep your business flourishing and one step ahead of the competition.
Habit 4	**R**	**REDUCE** reactivity and nurture proactivity. Turn conflict to contrast. Mindfulness practices cultivate calmness and contemplation. Making mindful choices usually shifts potentially volatile interactions into thoughtful and fruitful exchanges.
Habit 5	**E**	**ENCOURAGE** community over competitiveness and create a cohesive, connected work environment. Build relationships based on generosity. If your business has been based on the old win-lose paradigm, you can shift it to a system that activates and incentivizes cooperation.

Habit 6	S	**SHIFT** perception from selfishness to self-fullness. Create organic loyalty that supports care for both staff and customers. When staff truly care for themselves, they will be healthier and happier. Care for your business and your clients will organically follow.
Habit 7	E	**EMBRACE** diversity in the workplace through education, awareness, and conscious, interactive engagement. Prejudice comes from ignorance. Education and interaction support diversity and dispel narrow-mindedness.
Habit 8	N	**NEUTRALIZE** negativity through emotional intelligence (EI), training, and conscious communication. Cultivate calm in order to inspire productivity and prosperity. Building a culture that is committed to cooperative, constructive, and harmonious interplay creates true intimacy and naturally builds cohesion and team spirit.
Habit 9	T	**THANK** all support channels, and invoke the 3 T's: *trust, transformation,* and *treasure*. Shifting from worry to gratitude is a game changer. Once you gain trust in your staff, products, and Good Morning strategies, your business will exponentially transform. Treasure what you have, and further growth will follow!

Habit 1

BUILD a Solid Foundation Based on Honor and Integrity

To honor your staff is to trust that they will deliver their best. Cultivate a sense of security and self-appreciation in them and then give them the space to blossom.

Do you honor yourself, who you are, and what you have accomplished? I believe that we are all epic heroes in the journey of our lives. Each of us have extraordinary stories to tell—lives fraught with heartbreak and courage, pathos and passion. We are quick to dismiss who we are and what we have been through. We worship celebrities and stars because we fail to recognize the star that is within each of us. When we dismiss ourselves, we also tend to dismiss others. Our coworkers often tread lightly around us for fear of angering the fallen star that we embody. Cultivating honor and integrity begins within us. As we start to shine within our own eyes, we give permission to those around us to do the same.

I recently read a LinkedIn post by author Brigette Hyacinth:

> My new employee asked me to work from home. Then she started to tell me the reason. I told her, "No need to apologize and I don't need to know the details." I do not pay for seat warmers—to come to the office, fine. 9 to 5? Fine. Work from home. Fine. Work from the garage while they fix your car? Fine. I don't need to know you will be late because of a doctor's appointment, or you are leaving early to attend a personal matter. Everybody works at a different pace. You choose how to get your work done. It's sad how we have infantilized the workplace so much, that employees feel the need to apologize for having personal lives. I am not a clock watcher. I trust you to get your job done. Keep clients happy. I am happy. The future lies in flexible work patterns.

I love Brigette's attitude, and I have been graced to be managed similarly throughout my myriad of careers. Most employment opportunities I had were built on honor and integrity. After graduating from Queen's University in Kingston, Ontario, in 1985, I was offered a job in the marketing division at Big Blue—IBM. While I had worked many part-time jobs, IBM was my first full-time career placement.

What I remember most about the company was its merit system. It was clearly based on quality of work rather than tenure. Time and again, ambitious, talented staff would be promoted before other staff members who had been there longer but did not have as much talent. I felt recognized for my skills and highly supported. In fact, when I left Big Blue after a couple of years to pursue my acting dreams, they were remarkably accommodating. I was cast in a show that would take me to the stunning Four Seasons Minaki Lodge, located up in northwestern Ontario, for a six-month stint. Acting was my dream, and I explained that to my boss and to my boss's boss. Instead of threatening or discouraging me, they told me that they would provide me with the six months' leave. They assured me that their door was open and they would welcome me back if I decided to return. Although I never did, I always remember how they treated me and the encouraging terms under which I left.

Honor Profile

You may be surprised to learn how much you avoid honoring who you are and your accomplishments. This profile will give you greater perspective on this question, so that you can behave more honorably toward yourself and those who work with you. For each of the questions below, choose the number that most closely aligns with your current views, mindset, or situation (1 being "not at all" and 10 being "a great deal").

1. Do you believe that honoring self and others is central to who you are?

1 — 2 — 3 — 4 — 5 — 6 — 7 — 8 — 9 — 10

2. How much do those who work with you believe that you honor them?

1 — 2 — 3 — 4 — 5 — 6 — 7 — 8 — 9 — 10

3. Do you give up your seat to pregnant women, injured persons, or the elderly when they are in need?

1 — 2 — 3 — 4 — 5 — 6 — 7 — 8 — 9 — 10

4. Do you honor those who have served their country?

1 — 2 — 3 — 4 — 5 — 6 — 7 — 8 — 9 — 10

5. Do you honor the earth and its keepers?

1 — 2 — 3 — 4 — 5 — 6 — 7 — 8 — 9 — 10

6. Would your family members say that you are honorable towards them?

1 — 2 — 3 — 4 — 5 — 6 — 7 — 8 — 9 — 10

7. Do you do what is right and honorable rather than what best serves you?

1 — 2 — 3 — 4 — 5 — 6 — 7 — 8 — 9 — 10

8. Do you honor animals and insects, large and small?

1 — 2 — 3 — 4 — 5 — 6 — 7 — 8 — 9 — 10

9. Did your parents instill honor as an important trait within you?

1 — 2 — 3 — 4 — 5 — 6 — 7 — 8 — 9 — 10

10. Do you act honorably when no one is looking?

1 — 2 — 3 — 4 — 5 — 6 — 7 — 8 — 9 — 10

If you scored between 76 and 100, you have developed into a very honorable person. You see the inherent value in yourself and in others as well. You strive to recognize others and their value, and you make people feel respected and appreciated. Continue to develop even more honor towards yourself and watch it naturally increase towards others as well.

If you scored between 51 and 75, you have done a great deal to honor yourself and others. While you can still develop even greater honor in all you say and do, know that you have already come a long way in doing so. Pay attention to the times where you are dishonoring yourself or others. Don't judge yourself when you do so. Simply take note and commit to continuing to develop honor within you.

If you scored between 26 and 50, you have done some work towards honoring yourself and others, but you still have a way to go. Take an inventory of the areas in which you are lacking in honor. Once you are aware of these, you can begin to shift your commitment towards greater honor and respect for yourself and for others.

If you scored between 10 and 25, you still have quite a journey ahead to instill greater honor into your life. The first step is to honor yourself for your honesty in filling out this profile. The fact that you have rated yourself low indicates that you are honest about your challenges and are willing to look your issues square in the face. Know this, and commit to integrating honor into the way you treat yourself and others.

By completing this profile, you have gained a better understanding of where honor lies among the priorities in your life. Alongside honor is respect. Any relationship that lacks honor and respect lacks the building blocks of greater intimacy. Commit to honoring yourself and others more, and see how it is often returned twofold.

Honor Trigger Situation

Simon held a position as a plant manager in the furniture industry. Managing a plant was no easy feat. It required dedication, diplomacy, and people skills. He had all of these, along with the emotional intelligence required to support management, the staff, himself, and ultimately the customer. One day he noted a slowdown in production between the sewing department and packaging. When he asked the sewing manager, Marta, what the glitch was, she told him that two hours earlier one of the sewing machines had broken down.

The Ego's Response

Had Simon lacked the insights and communication skills necessary to alleviate the problem, there could have been a major blowout at the plant over this issue. As the plant manager, he was responsible for overall productivity, and his job was on the line. From the ego or mind's perspective, his initial thoughts might have been centered around the concern that Marta made him look bad in the eyes of higher management.

As Simon noted the slowdown, he could have started an accusatory dialogue:

> **Simon:** Marta, Why didn't you tell me about the broken sewing machine two hours ago, when it happened? How many times do I have to tell you to come to me immediately? Your tardiness is costing this company a great deal of money. (Note the condescending tone. He is attacking and shaming her in front of all of the staff, as opposed to speaking to her privately.)

> **Marta:** I didn't have time to tell you. We're working double time here. You and your management team drive us to the point of exhaustion. You can't get blood from a carrot, you know! What more do you want?

> **Simon:** No excuses. What kind of supervisor are you? You're going to cost me my job here, and I'm not going to tolerate any backtalk.

Marta: You're more worried about yourself and your job than you are about the well-being of your staff. Why the hell should we work so hard when you and the owners sit idly in your offices, making loads of money while we work our tails off on the hot warehouse floor all day, barely making ends meet?

Simon: You think I'm sitting idly? You have no idea what stresses I have. I'd trade jobs with you any day. And who do you think you are talking to me this way? This time you have gone too far.

Marta: No, I haven't gone far enough. Who needs this?

Simon: I don't need this, nor does this company. You're fired.

Marta: Good riddance. I'm out of here!

Simon could then have drawn up a scathing report and submitted it to the factory owner. The report might have read:

Marta did not report a broken sewing machine, and her apathy slowed down productivity. When I approached her about it, she was highly argumentative. She was not open to hearing the suggestions I made, and in fact threw a disrespectful temper tantrum for all of the staff to see. I had no recourse but to fire her.

This ego-based reaction could have set in motion a myriad of repercussions. First, staff morale would have been lowered as all watched the toxic exchange between Simon and Marta. Staff would fear a similar explosive interaction should they make an error in judgment. Marta could have lodged a complaint with the union, or she could have hired a lawyer to defend her in an expensive lawsuit. Production would have slowed further while the company sought out a replacement for Marta, and they could have fallen further behind. They would have lost still more time training her replacement. All of this would have cost a great deal of time, effort, and money.

The Heart's Response

In this case Simon responds to the situation in a more proactive way. He starts all initiatives and interactive engagement with a question that is rooted in his heart: "How may I serve?" He makes a deliberate intention to set aside his ego's worries and fears and work from a higher place. After establishing that change had to happen with Marta and her staff, he sets in motion a chain of events that becomes a win-win for all:

1. The first thing he does is ask Marta if he could speak to her in private. He is not immediately reactive to the situation and is thoughtful and intentional in his response. He schedules a meeting with Marta the following day. In the meantime, he does some research and sets a plan in motion.

2. The next day Simon approaches Marta not from a place of condemnation, but from a place of encouragement:

Simon: Good morning, Marta. How are you doing? (He first checks in with her emotionally and allows her to be heard. This is very important in any staff communication.)

Marta: I'm doing OK. To be honest, I'm a little worried about the fact that you called me into your office.

Simon: First of all, I want you to know that I appreciate how hard you work for this company. I know that you and your staff put in a lot of hours. (This sets the tone for the discussion that follows. Making positive statements about Marta's work ethic offset any defensiveness she may have been feeling. It also sets the tone for a positive and constructive conversation to ensue.) Before I go any further, I want to check in with you. Do you have anything you want to share with me? Any concerns or issues you are having? (He shows further concern for Marta and lets her know that he is there to support her.)

Marta: I'm glad you noticed how hard we work. Thanks for the vote of confidence. Issues? Nothing major. Things have pretty well been status quo. It took a while for the three new girls to catch on, but I think they're almost up to speed.

I'm a little concerned about a few of my girls. They are taking a lot of smoking breaks, and I am not only worried about productivity, but I am concerned about their health as well. Anyway, it's obvious why you called me in. I'm sorry about not telling you about the sewing machines earlier. I just got so busy and I didn't anticipate that we would get so far behind. (By asking Marta about any concerns, he has given her a chance to raise the issue of the broken machine. This puts her in a place of self-accountability and ownership. She feels more empowered by being the one to broach the subject).

Simon: Thanks for sharing your concern about the smoking. I'll give it some thought and see what I can come up with. Listen, Marta. I can fully understand being overwhelmed. I get the same way at times. That being said, do you feel safe coming to me? Is there anything that I can do in the future to ensure that this does not happen again? (By taking ownership and being open to feedback, Simon creates a stronger sense of safety for Marta.)

Marta: No. It's nothing you did or didn't do. At times we are so busy we just don't have a time to stop. When we do, we have to race out to the food truck to grab coffee and snacks. I just wish we had more time! I'm so sorry. It won't happen again!

Simon: Thanks, Marta. While I appreciate that, I see that something has to change. I'm going to do a little brainstorming and see what I can come up with. And please, if you have any ideas or further concerns, please don't hesitate to discuss them with me.

Marta: Many thanks, Simon. I will!

Simon lists the issues that Marta mentioned, along with the incident, and researches some resolutions. He calls Marta into his office a few days later.

Simon: Hi, Marta. I did a bit of research about the situations we previously discussed, and I have to say that I'm really excited! I think they were all catalysts to some real growth opportunities for the staff and for the company. I've been doing a little work on how to boost productivity, along with improving staff morale. Would you like to hear more?

Marta: Absolutely!

Simon then describes the plan, which includes:

1. An additional sewing machine available to immediately replace any machine that might break down in the future.

2. A program to help staff stop smoking. While in the beginning it costs the company money, in the end

it leads to a significant decrease in smoking (and smoking breaks) among the staff, which eventually affects the company's bottom line in an encouraging and profitable way.

3. An improved staff lounge area, with a station for coffee and tea having an upbeat, cheery decor.

4. A basketball hoop and a treadmill to encourage exercise among staff.

5. Stocking the fridge in the office with cold water, juice, and soda for staff.

6. A break time accrual incentive program. Staff are encouraged to take the allowed break time each day. However, every month, department heads submit records of break time taken by their staff. At the end of each month, the department with the least break time (above and beyond what is regulatorily allowable) receives a free pizza lunch.

7. Ongoing department-head brainstorming meetings that encourage nonjudgmental sharing and promote innovative approaches to staff-management relations and other areas of the business. The energy in these meetings is not in any way punitive. Open and honest sharing is supported and encouraged.

Marta responded enthusiastically. This plan gave a message to staff that management cared for their well-being. While some initiatives cost the company initially, in the long run the benefits far outweigh the costs. Supporting staff, as Simon did in this case, increases employee satisfaction and loyalty. This in turn decreases the "us versus them" mentality among workers and creates a more positive work environment.

The Witness-self's Response

Had Simon's consciousness been elevated to the level of the witness-self, he may have responded much as the heart-self did. But his state of consciousness might have been so heightened that he had a prior inkling about the broken sewing machine—what I would call a *preaction*. While this may sound absurd, when you are totally present and tapped into the creative force of source energy, your inner knowing becomes highly acute. You learn to hear the messages that most of us ignore. In this state, Simon may have gotten an inkling that the sewing machine was faulty even before it broke down. In response, he might have had a second machine already on hand to prevent any slowdown in productivity.

In any event, Simon would not have fretted about the loss of production time. While he would certainly address it, he would not have experienced it as a threat in any way. He would have noted it as a part of the ebb and flow of life as it passes through his conscious-ness. In other words, he would have been completely trusting that all would work out as it should. While he would have to respond and take the necessary actions to address the issue, he would not have been shaken in any way. He would not have lost any energy in response to it.

Innovative Implementation Ideas

- Have employee honoring events that celebrate each staff member and how they contribute to the success of the business.

- Conduct brainstorming sessions with department heads, encouraging creative ideas for supporting staff ease, innovativeness, and staff-management relationships.

- Offer a fun honor board activity luncheon or two. At these luncheons staff are given supplies to build honor boards, which they fill with quotes, photos, magazine pictures, and other decorations. These boards reflect the ways in which staff members respect and honor themselves.

- Train management how to communicate effec-tively, especially in providing constructive input for staff.

- Teach the Constructive Feedback Sandwich technique to your leadership staff: They should start each feedback session with a positive comment about the staff member's work. They go on to describe an area of potential improvement, using positive words, then end the conversation with a word of appreciation about another task that the employee does well.

Like disease in an ailing tree, lack of integrity rots us from the roots. Many of us lie to ourselves and have no idea that we are even doing so. We have to set a strong intention for inner integrity, and then we have to be willing to take a peek when it rears its ugly head. Then and only then can we release disease and heal ourselves and our businesses completely.

Coach Nagy Models Integrity

In the fall of 2019, after the Chicago Bears lost their final game of the season, I heard a radio interview with coach Matt Nagy, and I was greatly impressed. He took total responsibility for the loss. He did not make excuses, nor did he undermine his team's players or opponents. This was a shining example of inner integrity. While the responsibility for the Bears loss was not all his, he claimed it fully and publicly for all to hear. That kind of leadership builds deep respect among the players and encourages them to embody the same kind of integrity.

To display that kind of integrity, one has to have done a great deal of emotional work. To start, you have to commit to seeing all aspects of yourself. You have to be willing to face the untruths that you created to protect yourself from seeing aspects of your personality that you are not comfortable with.

To gain greater insight, fill out this Inner Integrity Profile.

Inner Integrity Profile

Committing to inner integrity will vastly improve your respect for yourself and in turn your respect for others (as well as theirs for you). The more you model integrity, the more those around you (including your employees) will follow suit. For each of the questions below, choose the number that most closely aligns with your current situation (1 being "not at all" and 10 being "a great deal").

1. Do you try to remain honest and truthful in all that you say and do?

1 — 2 — 3 — 4 — 5 — 6 — 7 — 8 — 9 — 10

2. Are your friendships based on honesty and honor rather than on gossip and exaggeration?

1 — 2 — 3 — 4 — 5 — 6 — 7 — 8 — 9 — 10

3. Do you run your business without perpetuating mistruths in order to achieve success?

1 — 2 — 3 — 4 — 5 — 6 — 7 — 8 — 9 — 10

4. Do you believe your staff possesses integrity and honesty?

1 — 2 — 3 — 4 — 5 — 6 — 7 — 8 — 9 — 10

5. Do you do your tax returns accurately and honestly?

1 — 2 — 3 — 4 — 5 — 6 — 7 — 8 — 9 — 10

6. If you are overpaid by someone, do you inform them and return the excess?

1 — 2 — 3 — 4 — 5 — 6 — 7 — 8 — 9 — 10

7. Do you sometimes catch yourself lying to yourself or others? If so, do you note it and try to change the behavior?

1 — 2 — 3 — 4 — 5 — 6 — 7 — 8 — 9 — 10

8. Do you place relationships above financial gain?

1 — 2 — 3 — 4 — 5 — 6 — 7 — 8 — 9 — 10

9. Are you willing and able to own your mistakes and openly and readily apologize for them?

1 — 2 — 3 — 4 — 5 — 6 — 7 — 8 — 9 — 10

10. Do you respect yourself and those who work for or with you?

1 — 2 — 3 — 4 — 5 — 6 — 7 — 8 — 9 — 10

If you scored between 76 and 100, you have already come a long way in developing your inner integrity. The more you commit to integrity, the more you will uncover additional areas where you are out of alignment—ways that might surprise you. When you do, be gentle with yourself and credit yourself for how far you have already come. Know in your heart that committing to inner integrity is one of the most fulfilling things you could do for yourself, your employees, and your business.

If you scored between 51 and 75, you have made vast strides in your commitment to live with integrity from the inside out. Once you set an intention to delve deeper, areas where you are not in integrity will be revealed to you. You will continue to gain insights that will further align you with your best self, and your staff will take note. Observe without judgment when you are not in integrity. Witness the truth when it is revealed to you, and allow it to inform the present and direct the future.

If you scored between 26 and 50, you have taken some steps towards inner integrity. Continue on your journey of self-discovery, knowing that it can be a tough pill to swallow. Seeing ourselves for who we are—the good, the bad, and the ugly—can be daunting, so it is important to treat your errors as you would treat a child who has gone off course. The same goes for your staff. Choose to express compassion and encourage deeper honesty in the future. This will prevent yourself and your staff from experiencing the shame of self-criticism.

If you scored between 10 and 25, you have a great deal to explore in the area of your inner integrity. See this not as condemnation, but as a sign that you are more aware and are moving in the right direction. If you are struggling to see how you are wanting in inner integrity, practice opening your heart and seek deeper revelation. Note times when you find yourself or your staff defensive. Often defensiveness is a sign of discomfort with our apparent failings. Avoid defending your defensiveness. Become still, and look boldly within yourself for the answers.

Now that you have a greater understanding of your own inner integrity, you can work towards developing it in yourself and your business. Doing so will build the morale of your employees and win you esteem in your industry, business partnerships, and customer base.

Integrity Trigger Situation

Thom had been employed at the publishing company for quite some time. Years before, another employee, who had since left, successfully developed and grew the department that Thom now leads.

At this point the company was struggling and was seeking new angles for adding to the business. The company's president met with Thom and asked him to come up with inventive ways to build their customer base.

During a search through his files, Thom came across a complete catalogue of offerings that his predecessor had created. It was inventive, provocative, and well-written.

The Ego's Response

Unfortunately, Thom responded to his discovery from a place of ego. He placed his own desires for recognition and success above inner integrity. He researched the database and noted that the catalogue had not previously been used by the company. Once he noted this, he claimed it as his creation. He introduced it to the president, who approved it and gave the directive to publish it. In this case, while the project was considered a great success by all, because of Thom's lack of inner integrity, his choice reeked of inauthenticity, dishonesty, and unearned adulation.

The Heart's Response

Had Thom been following a path of inner integrity, he would have responded with honesty and from his heart. He would have told the president that he came across the piece, crediting the previous department head and her part in its creation. While he would not have received recognition for creating the catalogue, he would have gained greater respect towards himself.

The Witness-self's Response

If Thom had responded from the witness-self, he would have likely followed the heart's response, or better yet, he might have been stimulated by a new and even better concept that welled up within him. He would have followed the guidance that came from his awakened heart. He would have done what best served the company's needs from a place of higher knowing and complete surrender.

In the end, although Thom received external accolades, he responded from his egoic mind to his peril. The wisest and highest part of him was aware of his dishonesty, and this awareness (conscious or unconscious) weakened his self-esteem. The law of attraction asserts that what we experience in the outer world around us reflects our inner state. In the end, his lack of esteem would affect not only his sense of self but his relationship to others as well. If he could not trust in himself, he would be unable to fully trust in others. Deceit and dishonor would continue to grow around him and within him until he was willing to face his own dishonesty and self-deception.

Innovative Implementation Ideas

- Write a list of the ways in which you have chosen inner integrity throughout your life. As you continue to commit to living with integrity, continue to list the ways in which you have done so. Give yourself a pat on the back and honor your commitment.

- Encourage inner integrity among your staff. Award them for honesty, and model it yourself.

- Have quarterly inner integrity lunches in which staff are encouraged to share stories of how they or their loved ones have modeled integrity.

- Be willing to apologize when you are wrong, and remind staff that having the courage to admit that you are wrong is not a weakness but a strength that shows depth of character.

As you continue your journey towards greater inner integrity, life will reveal more and more layers of self-deception until you come to the place where you have stripped yourself of your self-imposed masks. You will continue to be surprised as more and more is revealed. You may realize that you are not who you think you are. However, when you commit to transform from a place of deep compassion, your realizations will bring greater love, respect, and appreciation into your life.

Habit 2

EMBOLDEN Your Staff
Encourage self-accountability, pride, and ownership.

Only when we have the confidence to own the torrent of our mistaken ways can we bask in the sunshine of our victories.

When I looked up the meaning of *embolden*, I found this definition: "to give someone the courage or confidence to behave in a certain way." In this context, emboldening your staff does not mean encouraging them to behave in a certain way. In fact, it is much the opposite. To embolden is to support them in finding their own courage, rooted in a deep sense of who they are and what they can accomplish. In doing so, they will perform well beyond behaving in a certain specified way. They will produce remarkable, even magical, results upon which you and your business can flourish.

I experienced this when directing theater productions. In the early 1990s, I was accepted by an MFA program in theater directing at Purdue University. It was a wonderful opportunity: I was given a full scholarship, and I was also paid to do research each month. I got a definitive sense of my directing style, and I got clarity on my ethical and artistic commitments. The more I watched other directors bully their actors during rehearsals, the more it became crystal clear to me how ineffective it was and how unwilling I was to go that route.

When I work with actors, I am committed to creating a safe and secure place so that they can feel creatively unencumbered. I believe that only then will they feel free to take chances and blossom into their creative best. During rehearsals, I always encourage the actors to make crazy, apparently insane choices. I suggest that they portray their characters in an opposite manner to what they believe is inherent in the script. When such freedom and flexibility are encouraged, the actors often come up with unexpected choices that are brilliant—choices that I myself would never have imagined. Time and again, magic has been made on the stage as the performers have always felt safe and creatively free.

The same approach is essential, whatever the workplace. By taking the five following steps, you will support your staff and embolden them towards greater ownership and self-respect.

1. Cultivate pride within your staff. Let them know you hired them because you saw their talents and potential. Then give them the resources, but also

the space, to hold themselves responsible and accountable for their choices.

2. Give your staff a sense of ownership. You can do so by:
   - Asking questions rather than providing answers, allowing employees to make discoveries on their own.
   - Empowering them to have the courage to admit that they are wrong and apologize. Explain that when they have the courage and insight to do so, you gain even more respect for them.

3. Practice active listening with employees. Let them take the lead in conversations, and let them know that you see and hear them.

4. Let your staff know how much you appreciate them. One can never feel too appreciated. But make sure that you are authentic in expressing gratitude.

5. Model ownership of your own errors. Commit to being transparent, and take care not to put yourself on a pedestal.

Creating that safe place for my actors was a very selfish move on my part. Doing so served my needs as well as theirs. Doing their best made me look good as a director. My selfishness created a win-win outcome!

Internal Empowerment Profile

Before delving further into how you can integrate Habit 2 into your business practices, take some time to do an Internal Empowerment Profile to learn how empowered you believe yourself to be. Power begets power. When you are empowered, you feel safe and secure enough to allow your workers to empower themselves. For each of the questions below, choose the number that most closely aligns with your current situation (1 being "not at all" and 10 being "a great deal").

1. Do you confidently follow your own inner guidance when making decisions?
1 — 2 — 3 — 4 — 5 — 6 — 7 — 8 — 9 — 10

2. Do others seek your advice when making decisions?
1 — 2 — 3 — 4 — 5 — 6 — 7 — 8 — 9 — 10

3. Are you impactful in your area of business?
1 — 2 — 3 — 4 — 5 — 6 — 7 — 8 — 9 — 10

4. Do you follow your inner guidance despite interference from others?
1 — 2 — 3 — 4 — 5 — 6 — 7 — 8 — 9 — 10

5. Did you stand your ground with your parents or guardians when you were growing up?
1 — 2 — 3 — 4 — 5 — 6 — 7 — 8 — 9 — 10

6. Are you unaffected by the criticism of others?

1 — 2 — 3 — 4 — 5 — 6 — 7 — 8 — 9 — 10

7. Do you dance to your own beat regardless of the status quo?

1 — 2 — 3 — 4 — 5 — 6 — 7 — 8 — 9 — 10

8. Do you forge new paths, allowing your creativity to move you?

1 — 2 — 3 — 4 — 5 — 6 — 7 — 8 — 9 — 10

9. Do you stand your ground after making an important decision?

1 — 2 — 3 — 4 — 5 — 6 — 7 — 8 — 9 — 10

10. Are you effective at delegating tasks to others?

1 — 2 — 3 — 4 — 5 — 6 — 7 — 8 — 9 — 10

If you scored between 76 and 100, congratulations! You feel very empowered and have developed a strong sense of who you are. You are confident, and your confidence is transferred to those around you. You are an excellent manager and leader. You are strong-willed, but confident enough to be flexible when necessary. You believe in others and allow them the trust and space to be their best selves.

If you scored between 51 and 75, you are quite self-empowered. You have already done a great deal of work to strengthen your trust in yourself. As you further develop confidence, you will create a greater sense of well-being and confidence among your staff. Make an effort towards delegating more tasks at the workplace, allowing staff the space and the confidence to step into their true power.

If you scored between 26 and 50, you have done some work to empower yourself, but there is a great deal more opportunity for growth in this area. Take time to acknowledge yourself and avoid underestimating all that you have accomplished in your life. Also acknowledge your staff for their contributions, no matter how small. Doing so will build their confidence and create a greater sense of well-being in the workplace.

If you scored between 10 and 25, you are feeling quite disempowered. First, congratulate yourself for having the insight to see this. Take some time to list all of the things (big and small) that you have accomplished in your life. Then note the ways in which you have touched the lives of others, empowering and encouraging them to be their best. Offer yourself the same acknowledgment, and commit to stepping fully into your power.

Self-accountability

Self-accountability takes great courage. Like the willow, one who possesses self-accountability will build strong, deep roots and branches that are malleable and bendable so that they can withstand the greatest of storms.

The first of the three aspects of empowerment that we are going to look at is self-accountability. Taking ownership of what we do, be it good or bad, takes a great deal of confidence. If as an employee I take an inventory of my skills, I am clear on how I can best serve the company. However, if I am insecure and lacking in confidence, I will avoid looking at my weaknesses, fearing that I will be defined as broken or weak.

Self-accountability Trigger Situation

Sandy just cast Holmes in the starring role of Nathan Detroit in her upcoming production of *Guys and Dolls*. He is a triple threat, with a strong voice, excellent dance skills, and acting talent. To top it all off, he has exceptional onstage charisma.

Holmes showed up twenty-minutes late for the first read-through of the script. Later, when Sandy asked him why, he said that he needed to assist a friend in need and missed his bus. He assured her that it would not happen again. Unfortunately, Holmes continued to show up late for several of the practices.

The Ego's Response

If both Sandy and Holmes responded to the situation from the level of the mind or ego, they would have both been defensive and reactive. The conversation might have gone like this:

> **Sandy:** Holmes, you have been late for every single rehearsal. When you do a show, it's not just

you on the stage. You're letting down the entire cast and crew. What do you have to say for yourself? (Condemning him in front of the cast, she publicly shames him.)

Holmes: You're exaggerating. I haven't been late for *every* rehearsal. Look, it's impossible to get here when you call us so early in the morning. Buses only run every half hour, and damned if I'm going to sit around waiting for twenty minutes before rehearsals start. (Holmes counters by calling Sandy on her exaggeration. He sees himself as a victim to her early call times and the transit system.)

Sandy: Think about it, Holmes. You could use the twenty-minute wait time to memorize your lines. It'd do you some good. In fact, showing up early for a change would do us all some good! If you don't start smartening up, I'm going to have to recast your part and let you go. (Sandy uses sarcasm to belittle him and then threatens him with the possibility of firing him.)

Holmes: Give me a break, Sandy. This "fun" musical is becoming a drag! And I'm not the only one who thinks so. (Holmes attacks Sandy for not being supportive—again failing to take ownership and positioning himself as a victim to her insensitivity. He then tries one-upping her by claiming that others collude with his criticism of her.)

Sandy: Oh, really? Well, if others feel the same, then why don't they speak up? Are you all cowards? If you've got something to say, say it to my face! (Sandy responds defensively and attacks the entire cast.)

Holmes: They're not going to, because you're not approachable. They're all afraid of you. (Holmes attacks Sandy further, stating that all are victims and that she is cold and difficult to deal with).

Sandy: You know what, Holmes? I've just about had enough of you. You're fired. (Sandy pulls rank and publicly fires him.)

Holmes: Fine. Good luck finding somebody else who can do my role at this stage of the game. Lady, you're screwed! (Holmes retaliates by threatening her.)

Sandy: There's plenty more where you came from. You're one of thousands of talented guys. (Sandy tries to attack Holmes' self-esteem, claiming he is one of many and in no way special.)

Holmes: You think so? Well, good luck to you, Ms. Cool Cat! (Holmes gets the final word in, attacking Sandy as cold and insensitive.)

You can see how both parties were reactive towards one another. They were both guarded and communicating from their egos instead of their hearts. They both disempowered themselves, maintaining that they were victims of the other's shortcomings. This dialogue was toxic and did nothing to effect positive change. In fact, with the entire cast not only privy to the conversation, but actually brought into the attack, it will take a great deal of emotional healing to mend the wounds that were opened during this exchange.

The Heart's Response

Responding to the same situation with an open heart would create a much more positive outcome. In this scenario, Sandy quietly approaches Holmes as he shows up late, and she pulls him aside.

> **Sandy:** Hey, Holmes, can I have a word with you after rehearsal is through? Let's meet up in the sound booth, OK? (She is calm and not reactive. She quietly takes him aside and does not openly shame him.)

> **Holmes:** OK.

> **Sandy (after rehearsal, in the sound booth):** Holmes, I noticed you were late for rehearsal today, and it's happened a couple of other times. Is there something up that you want me to know about? (Sandy does not exaggerate Holmes' tardiness. She shows concern and asks an open-ended question, as opposed to verbally attacking him.)

Holmes: No. (Holmes does not feel attacked, so he does not counterattack. He doesn't feel safe enough to speak yet.)

Sandy notes Holmes' trepidation and delves further, but does so using verbiage that is supportive rather than attacking:

Sandy: I see a potential pattern here, and I want to help you out. I think you are an incredibly talented actor, and I would hate to see tardiness put a damper on your career. You've got too much going for you. Is there anything I can do to help you get to rehearsals on time? (Sandy affirms Holmes' talent and genuinely and supportively asks how she can help.)

Holmes: Yeah! Come to my house with an early morning cappuccino in hand and drag my sorry butt out of bed! (Holmes is awkward and uses humor to defuse the situation. But he does not deny his lateness, nor does he attack Sandy.)

Sandy: Seriously, Holmes, what's the problem? This pattern doesn't seem to fit with the disciplined singer and dancer I see onstage. (Sandy redirects the conversation back to the issue at hand. She gives Holmes the benefit of the doubt and encourages him again by pointing out that she has noted him as a disciplined performer.)

Holmes: Truth is, I am oblivious to alarms. I just don't hear them. I'm a deep sleeper. I set sixteen alarms to get me out of bed, and I still don't hear them. I don't know what you or anyone can do. (Holmes feels safe and lets his guard down. He owns his tardiness and opens up to why he is often late.)

Sandy: Hey, I have an idea. Beth lives up the way from you, and she's an early bird. What if you ask her to drop by your place on her way so she can drag your sorry butt out of bed? Would that help? (Sandy counters with a creative solution.)

Holmes: Absolutely, if she's game.

Sandy: Maybe she can pick up a cup of coffee for both you on her way to your place . . . and you can offer to buy. Sound like a plan? (Sandy offers a way in which there would be reciprocity for Holmes.)

Holmes: Sure!

Sandy: As for the long term, have you ever had sleep tests done? Sometimes if you suffer from sleep apnea, you have a difficult time waking up. You might just look into a sleep study sometime. (Sandy further offers a long-term suggestion, showing that she cares and wants the best for Holmes.)

Holmes: Thanks. I might just do that.

Sandy: I think we've got a plan, Holmes. As the director, I'm here to support you. Please know that you can also come to me when issues arise. (Sandy makes herself further available to Holmes and creates a dynamic that is based on support over attack and resolution over conflict.)

Holmes: Thanks, Sandy. I really appreciate your support, and I'm excited to finally get things on track.

This conversation clearly had a much better outcome than the first. In this case, Sandy was warm and supportive, and she stayed away from reactively attacking Holmes. While she had reason to be angry, she knew that approaching him with the intention "Let's work on this together. How may I help?" would be far more fruitful.

In response, Holmes took ownership of his tardiness. This does not always happen. In another scenario, he might never have taken responsibility for his actions. He might have maintained a defensive attack stance throughout the conversation. Nonetheless, when the manager creates a safe place in which resolution is the intention, the worker is more inclined to let down their guard and have an honest conversation.

I have experienced this countless times as a corporate trainer. During my training sessions, I do a role play with staff members. On numerous occasions afterward, they have told me that they tried to maintain aggression and anger, but because my heart was open and my position was that of compassion and service, they could not do so.

Being nonreactive and committing to maintaining a proactive, problem-solving stance takes discipline, but you will find that it is well worth the effort. Of course, if your staff continue to be irresponsible and ornery after several warnings, then further action, like termination, may be necessary.

The Witness-self's Response

If Sandy was responding from the witness-self, she would possess great compassion for Holmes. This does not mean that she would blindly accept his behavior, but she would coach him through the issue in a way that was so deeply understanding that he would feel completely and utterly supported. Any defensiveness he may have had at the beginning of the conversation would melt away. With Sandy's deeper compassion, Holmes might have honored and respected her more than anyone else he had ever encountered. He would have been drawn to her heightened state.

The light of Sandy's inner flame would inspire Holmes and others. The right jobs would come her way frequently and easily. She would see apparent obstacles as opportunities and would in no way resist anything that came her way. She would support others by simply being in her awakened state.

Pride

To say "I can do better" is actually a subtle form of
arrogance. Root yourself in pride, and from
there you will naturally find true humility.

The second aspect of empowerment we will be discussing is pride. As I was doing my own work around pride and inner authenticity in the theater, I came to a startling realization: when someone complimented me on a performance, I would shrug off the compliment with a comment like "I could have done . . ." or "I didn't do . . ."

At the time, I thought I was being humble. However, upon further internal investigation, I realized that my self-depreciation was actually a form of arrogance. I was saying, "What you saw was not my best. I am better." I was shocked! Now when I receive a compliment about a performance, I simply respond with a "Thank you" and leave it at that.

To provide some clarity on arrogance, I believe that many of us have it backwards. We believe that arrogant people think better of themselves than others, but in fact it is the exact opposite. Whenever I feel insecure, I push my "I'm so good" verbiage onto others (usually in the form of "She said this about me . . ." or "The reviewer said I was . . ."). I would list all of the kudos I received to convince others that I am good at what I do. Why? Because in my heart of hearts, I don't

really believe that I am! If I did, I would have no need
to boast. I would sit comfortably and confidently with
my inner knowing.

I am fascinated with those who have cultivated
deep humility. It is a trait that I want to nurture more
in my life. While I am far from embodying it, I have
noted that those who are most humble are individuals
who see themselves as a part of a larger divine plan.
They do not regard their feats as theirs, but they see
themselves as mere vessels through which prowess
and creativity are channeled.

Rooting Yourself and Your Staff in Pride

Acknowledging yourself and your staff for work well
done is in no way harmful. Some business owners are
concerned that providing staff with too much encouragement can backfire. They fear their workers will
grow arrogant and place more demands upon the
management. However, when pride is fostered from
within, your employees have no need to seek external
accolades. Their sense of self-worth is unshakable.

Ownership

*Own your successes and failures, and give others
permission to own theirs. Know that in every moment we
are all doing our best. If we knew better, we would do better.*

The third aspect of employee empowerment is ownership. When I was hired at Nightingale-Conant

Corporation, management had an easygoing sensibility. When I first arrived at the job, they told me that they wanted me to head up a personal coaching program with psychic Sonia Choquette. I remember my first day. They showed me to my office, and that was that. No one stood over me to show me the ropes. I was left to fend for myself. Management assumed that if I had questions, I would ask—and when I had any, I did.

My first step was to study Sonia's book *Psychic Pathways* and set up a coaching program based on it. After taking some seminars with Sonia, I noted that she encouraged us all to use our intuitive abilities. She said that we all had intuition and that it was a matter of trusting and cultivating it. I began to play with my intuition, and I discovered that the more I explored it, the more it grew. Developing it and watching it flourish was extremely exciting and a great deal of fun.

My first step was to write an advertising mailer to promote Sonia's three-month coaching program. Did I have any previous experience in copywriting? No, but I worked on tapping into the mindset of the reader. I went to the curious seeker within me and wrote from the perspective of what my wants and needs would be. To encourage readers to participate in the coaching program, I offered a free psychic profile. Sonia had created a profile questionnaire at the beginning of her book, so I used it to drive potential clients to return the mailer. Once they responded, I would take them through their psychic profile and then sell the three-month coaching program.

Before I knew it, a multitude of Sonia's fans had responded. My challenge was the way in which I had worded the ad copy. Many respondents thought that they were getting a psychic reading from Sonia herself. While I could not offer them a personal reading from her, I was able to stay within the parameters of her teachings. In response to her encouragement to play with our intuition, I began to facilitate the profiles and give intuitive readings to the clients who requested them. It was a great deal of fun and solidified my trust in the innate intuitive abilities that we all possess.

Nightingale management gave me ownership of Sonia's Psychic Pathway program, and I learned a great deal, including the practice of sharing my own intuitive senses with clients.

Innovative Implementation Ideas

- Create an annual showcase event where staff can each share their work progress. Liken this event to that of a science fair, where staff create fun displays and show off their abilities. Perhaps offer some prizes.

- Encourage staff to engage with their intuition. Commend them when they follow through on their gut responses, and acknowledge their courage for doing so.

- Have a monthly "This is me" session in which each staff member can spend fifteen minutes sharing their interests, their background, and their passions with coworkers. They would be encouraged to bring in photographs and memorabilia that would help coworkers to get to know them.

Habit 3

PLACATE Fear
Expel constrictive mindsets, build security, and ignite creative genius.

There are only two choices in life: fear and love. When a business is built on love, nothing fearful can find its way in!

Although many are oblivious to it, fear is an integral part of the human condition. I believe that many, if not all, of us are here to discover just how fearful we are. In seeing the fear, we can dig deeper into our hearts and feel greater compassion for ourselves and others. In time, as we witness the fear without judgment, our faith in the benevolence of the universe grows, and the fear begins to dissipate.

Unless dealt with, fear restricts, constricts, and tightens the muscle of any business. In time that muscle will be pulled and compromised. Rooted in a scarcity mindset, it wreaks havoc in our lives when it is not recognized and channeled. As you commit to looking honestly within yourself, you might discover more fearfulness than you ever realized.

Perfectionism as Fear

Years ago I was asked to do a mundane task for a teacher I was assisting at my daughter's school. She simply asked me to put notices in each of the children's mailboxes.

I had previously set a very strong intention, asking the universe to reveal to me the ways in which I had been deceiving myself. I especially wanted to focus on fears, as I was acutely aware of how much they were running my life. While many friends and colleagues would consider me fairly brave, I knew otherwise.

Much to my shock, as I was placing the notices in each mail slot, I noted that my abdomen was tightening up. I stopped and took a couple of breaths, asking myself what it was about. The fearful perfectionist deep within me revealed itself to me: I feared missing one of the slots. I was shocked to realize that I could experience fear over such a mundane task. But instead of judging myself, I responded from a place of appreciation at the insight. It provided me with an opportunity to see just how fearfully I had been living my life.

Fear is often at the heart of all of our woes. Once we realize this, we can speak to the fear, calming it and cultivating compassion for it. In the end, seeing it and fully experiencing it without resistance will help to heal it.

Fear Inventory Profile

As is evidenced by the realization I just shared, fear that may seem totally illogical can hide deep within us. Doing this Fear Inventory Profile will give you greater insight into how fearful you might be. For each of the questions below, choose the number that most closely aligns with your current situation (1 being "not at all" and 10 being "a great deal").

1. Are you open to veering into new directions when called to do so?

1 — 2 — 3 — 4 — 5 — 6 — 7 — 8 — 9 — 10

2. Do you welcome change and see it as a positive experience?

1 — 2 — 3 — 4 — 5 — 6 — 7 — 8 — 9 — 10

3. Do you stay away from watching fearful or violent events in the media?

1 — 2 — 3 — 4 — 5 — 6 — 7 — 8 — 9 — 10

4. In general, do you believe yourself and your family to be safe?

1 — 2 — 3 — 4 — 5 — 6 — 7 — 8 — 9 — 10

5. Do you trust that your business is protected and that there is no need to fear that negative situations will take it from you?

1 — 2 — 3 — 4 — 5 — 6 — 7 — 8 — 9 — 10

6. In general, do you believe that people are good?

1 — 2 — 3 — 4 — 5 — 6 — 7 — 8 — 9 — 10

7. Do you believe that the universe has your back?

1 — 2 — 3 — 4 — 5 — 6 — 7 — 8 — 9 — 10

8. Do you generally think positive thoughts throughout the day instead of brooding over negativity?

1 — 2 — 3 — 4 — 5 — 6 — 7 — 8 — 9 — 10

9. Do you experience fear but move through it anyway (as opposed to being paralyzed by it)?

1 — 2 — 3 — 4 — 5 — 6 — 7 — 8 — 9 — 10

10. Are you compassionate towards others when they are fearful?

1 — 2 — 3 — 4 — 5 — 6 — 7 — 8 — 9 — 10

If you scored between 76 and 100, congratulations! For the most part, you are aware of your fears and you don't allow them to rule your life. Your self-awareness has served you and your business well. Continue to explore the ways in which fear has a hold on you. As you do, you will learn to see it for what it is and develop the faith that your life and your business are unfolding the way they should.

If you scored between 51 and 75, you are quite aware of your fears, and you are able to function at a fairly high level of calm and security. As you continue to explore how fear manifests in your life, simply witness without judgment. Take note of times when you judge others and their fears. The more critical you are of them, the more fearful you are.

If you scored between 26 and 50, you have done some work with your fears and have opened the portal to deeper exploration. Make a commitment to step into your fears. When confronted with fear, note it and then take some action on the task despite the fear. Doing so will build your business. As you cultivate more courage, you will trust yourself and the benevolence of the universe more.

If you scored between 10 and 25, you have a wonderful opportunity to explore your fears further. For the most part, they are keeping you from fully manifesting your desires and could be blocking more success. Don't fear your fears. Step into them, noting that even tiny steps will eventually lead you to greater courage. Stay away from fear-inspiring media, and when you catch yourself experiencing fear, have a conversation with it and allow it to fully express itself. Doing so will provide you with greater insights and confidence.

Completing this profile will help you explore your fears and eventually embrace them. Unless you do so, fear will permeate your business and harm your decision making, your staff, and your exchanges with customers.

Replacing the Taskmaster

Many business owners believe that in order to run a successful business, you need to be a taskmaster with a firm grip on your staff. This is not the case. In fact it is counter to creating a thriving and lucrative work environment. If you hire the right staff and live by the tenets of the Good Morning Mind, you will create an environment of encouragement and positive expectations. You will discover that all of the cogs in the wheel of the business will work harmoniously to support it.

Fear-Based Trigger Situation

Annie worked part-time in the data preparation department of an international bank. She was a student. She was a go-getter and committed to doing her best, whatever the task. One of her jobs was to run a microfilming machine that took photos of credit card transaction forms. (This was long before the advent of the Internet, when we used to sign hard copy credit card forms that were then forwarded to the banks and filmed for recordkeeping.)

The task was very boring, and as Annie spent hours and hours sitting by the machine, she came up with some options that would speed up the process considerably. The standard routine was to stop the machine between each box, record numbers on the completed box, fill out the procedural tracking form, and then load the new box of forms onto the machine for processing. There would be about a five-minute delay between boxes. The entire process took twenty minutes per box. In order to quell her boredom and be more productive, Annie did not turn off the machine between boxes. She created a procedure where she could fulfil all tasks without doing so. By revising the procedure for a seven-hour shift, with each box taking only fifteen minutes to be filmed and processed, she was able to process seven additional boxes, for a total of twenty-eight. That's a great deal of increased productivity.

The bank, which was very structured, required Annie to record her hours and the number of boxes completed. She was honest and fastidious in doing so, but one day she was approached by her supervisor, John, about her time tracking sheet.

The Ego's Response

At the end of her shift, Annie submits her tracking sheet to John, who is sitting at his desk at the front of the data entry department. He does a quick review of it and then immediately starts the following conversation.

> **John:** Annie, we need to discuss your tracking sheets. I believe that you have been lying on them for quite some time. As you know, the company doesn't take lying lightly. (John immediately accuses Annie in front of her coworkers. He threatens her by stating that the company would not support the apparent lying.)

Annie: I wasn't lying! What are you talking about? (Annie immediately gets defensive as she feels attacked.)

John: Let's look at last Thursday's sheet. According to your numbers, you finished microfilming twenty-one boxes during the seven-hour shift. That's impossible! (Leaving no room for discussion, John attacks further.)

Annie: No, it's not. I was honest, and I don't appreciate being called a liar. I've been . . .

John: Let me finish, Annie. I'm sorry, but I'm going to have to take this to higher management and see what they have to say. I know you're obsessed with doing well, but lying about your productivity is taking it way too far! (John pulls rank and does not allow Annie to finish her statement. He criticizes her work ethic and again accuses her of lying.)

Annie: But I've found a new . . .

John: Annie, case closed. I've got way too much work to do, and I don't have time to argue this with you. It's all here in black-and-white. Higher management will be the judge. (John silences Annie and shames her by mentioning the workload that she is preventing him from completing. He escalates the situation without a two-way conversation with Annie).

Annie: But . . .

John: Enough. I'll call you once I've shown this to the department director. Now good night. (John silences Annie and abruptly ends the conversation.)

The Heart's Response

John approaches Annie at the beginning of her next shift. He heads to the room where she is getting ready to start microfilming. He is calm, thoughtful, and deliberate in his tone.

John: Hey, Annie, how are you doing? (Annie is the only person in the room, so John is speaking to her in private.)

Annie: Good.

John: I know you just finished exams. How's it all going? (John is warm and welcoming.)

Annie: Pretty good. I'm feeling quite confident about them.

John: Great! I know you're a hard worker. Listen, I want to bring something to your attention. I've noted recently on your time tracking sheet that you've been averaging about twenty-one boxes of microfilming in a seven-hour shift. That's pretty impressive. (John, giving Annie the benefit of the doubt, compliments her, setting her further at ease.)

Annie: Thank you!

John: I was wondering if you could explain to me how you manage to get so many boxes completed. (John continues to explore openly, without attacking or accusing Annie.)

Annie: Sure. I'm glad you asked. As you know, doing seven hours of microfilming can be pretty boring, so I'm always trying to find faster ways of doing things. I play a game where I work to beat the clock, so to say. (Annie, feeling safe and heard, shares her process with John.)

John: Sounds interesting. Tell me more!

Annie: Well, instead of stopping the machine between boxes, I keep it running and write out the number tracking and dispense the new boxes while the machine is in continuous motion.

John: Hmm. Can you show me how you do it? (John remains open and curious. He uses a calm and supportive tone of voice.)

Annie: Sure. I'd be glad to! (Annie proceeds to show John the technique that she uses.)

John: Wow, Annie. That's pretty impressive! I see you working super hard—you have to in order to keep things moving without stopping. (John compliments and encourages Annie.)

Annie: I do, but to be honest with you, it keeps me from getting too bored.

John: I see. Do you think you could teach your coworkers your technique? (John encourages Annie further. Instead of crediting himself, he asks her to step into more of a leadership role by teaching coworkers.)

Annie: Sure. I'd love to!

John: Thanks, Annie, and keep up the outstanding work. You are a great asset to the team, and I look forward to hiring you full-time during Christmas holidays and summers. (John ends the conversation on a high note and lets Annie know that she is valued in the organization.)

Annie: Thanks, John. You know, I get paid double what most of my friends get paid, and I'm so grateful. This place is paying for my education.

This heart-based conversation uplifted both employees. John learned of Annie's technique, and she felt validated. Annie was able to train her coworkers, and ultimately her technique saved the company a great deal of money. John submitted a bonus request at Christmas, and Annie received a nice check for her innovativeness. Had John chosen to lead the conversation with his ego, the company could have lost a top-notch employee and missed out on her valuable process.

The Witness-self's Response

John may have had an intrinsic knowing about Annie's process. Whether he did or not, he would have deeply appreciated her initiative and would have let her know that her efforts were recognized. He may have noted the wounded part of her that was overzealous and potentially exhausting herself. He may have compassionately but pointedly coached her to observe the part of herself that needs to overachieve.

For her part, at a very young age, Annie may have had an opportunity to heal the perfectionistic aspect of herself that drove her to overachieve instead of accepting ease and effortlessness in her work.

Build a Fortress, and Armies Will Attack

There is a saying: "When you build a fortress, armies will attack."

What does that mean? According to the law of attraction, when you expect and anticipate negativity, very often you draw it to you through your fear. If you believe that the world is a dangerous place, often you will experience it as such.

When I first arrived in Chicago, I heard all of the stories about the violence in the city, but after doing a lot of world travel, I learned to trust my personal danger radar and not focus on fear-based thinking. Once I got lost and found myself in a rundown part of town. I made no mind and had every intention of seeking out thoughtful people who could help me find my way home. I pulled over and asked a man who looked kind and approachable for directions. As expected, he knew his way around town and he set me on the right course home. When I arrived at home, I told my husband where I had gotten lost, and he gasped, "You stopped and asked for directions there? You are lucky you weren't shot!"

To be clear, I am not suggesting that you put yourself, your staff, or your business in harm's way. However, I am suggesting that what you focus your attention and energy on makes a difference.

Where You Build Security, Genius Follows

When you lead from the place of love, you build security among your employees. When they feel secure, their genius is ignited, innovation expands, and your business transforms vastly.

Consider the fearful stance. When you are in fear, the muscles in your body tighten and constrict, your heart beats more rapidly, and your adrenaline increases. You go into fight-or-flight mode. You expend a great deal of energy.

If you consider the stance of enthusiasm, you will note similar physiological traits. Here too your heart beats faster and your adrenaline increases, but your muscles don't necessarily tighten; your energy is expansive, and not in any way constricted. You have taken the "fight" out of the fight-or-flight equation. When this is the case, energy is raised as opposed to depleted, allowing your heart and mind to soar. Your enthusiasm is a catalyst for invention and innovation. As ideas are shared and supported, more ideas come to mind, producing a positive chain reaction.

Producing from the Heart

The famous director James Cameron once said, "Fortune favors the prepared." While I can't agree more, I would extend that sentiment to read, "Fortune favors the prepared, and provides bonuses for the bold."

As I previously mentioned, when I worked at Nightingale-Conant I was given free rein to complete my tasks as I saw fit. Throughout the many years there, I was never micromanaged or criticized for the unique way in which I went about my work. For many years I reported to Dan Strutzel, who was the vice president of publishing for the company. Dan was an exemplary leader and a joy to work with. I felt seen and appreciated by him, and I knew that he always had my back.

As an audiobook producer, I was responsible for writing outlines for the programs that I produced. I would build each session (or chapter) with a brief opening paragraph describing what would be covered, along with bullet point questions to ask the author. I would sit in the recording booth with the author and serve as the listener. Thus the recording was very fresh, in the moment and conversational. I would show them the outline, but I would also ask their permission to veer off of the outline into new territory if I felt compelled to do so. I would encourage the same of them. Thus, if a question, idea, or practical exercise arose that was not in the outline, we would run with it. To facilitate such flexibility, we both had to be fully present.

This bolder way of recording programs constantly fed us new ideas, techniques, and exercises that created a much better product.

Over a decade ago, I was privileged to record several audio programs with the late Dr. David Hawkins. He was an extraordinary man. During one of our first recordings, he invited his friend Niko to attend. Niko was a delightful man, and during one of the breaks, he shared a sacred Buddhist chant with us. The purity of his tone and his vocal resonance were remarkable. He created an energy that uplifted us all. At the end of the two-day session, I had an intuitive hit to pull Niko into the studio and record a session with him. I conducted an interview and recorded his divine chant.

Fast-forward over ten years, and I recently received a phone call from Niko. As is often the case, he had popped into my thoughts a couple of days before he called, so when he did, I was not surprised. He thanked me for recording him and told me that he had received millions of responses on social media. Since the recording, he has been requested to present at several events. He thanked me, saying that the recording changed his life.

Although my ego would love to take responsibility for the choice I made, I was not the instigator. There was a voice, I'll call it, from within me that beckoned me to call him into the recording session. When you live in fear, either you don't hear that voice or you choose to ignore it on the grounds that it doesn't make logical sense. But I believe that innovation, creativity, and genius trump logic.

Next time you or your staff members get an intuitive hit, I encourage you to follow through on it. They come from Source and offer an outcome that far outweighs our logical, predictable, and often fear-based plans.

In fact, I encourage you to conduct creative brainstorming meetings among all staff at least once a month. Once I wrote a study guide for a recording by innovation leader Doug Hall. At the time, he had a retreat center called the Eureka Ranch, where Fortune 500 CEOs and other thought leaders would go and literally play. From their playtime, these corporate leaders would come up with the most innovative, ingenious ideas. You don't have to go to Eureka Ranch to encourage innovation in your business (although it's on my bucket list to attend someday). Set an intention for joyful and playful collaboration in the workplace. Encourage innovation and out-of-the-box thinking from all of your staff, and watch as your business takes flight!

Build Security

Without security, our creativity hides in the closet
of our subconscious, and all of the monsters
of our youth come to life.

When I lived in Vancouver, I did some television work. The difference between mindsets at the various auditions was potent and palpable. When I auditioned for an "actor" role (five lines or less), the actors were intense and agitated and often displayed a great deal of fear. They were frantically preparing for their audition, running lines in their heads, asking other actors to read with them, and so on.

On the other hand, when I was called in for a "principal" role (six lines or more), the energy in the room was completely different. These more seasoned performers were not frantically preparing for their auditions. There was a sense of calm and confidence in the room. The actors were laughing and engaging with one another. Not one individual was frantically looking over his or her script, lost in a spiral of fear.

When I noted this distinction, I was at first surprised and then convinced: what separated the pros from the less experienced was calm and confidence. The pros were secure in their abilities and acted accordingly.

Security Trigger Situation

Garrett got a job as a learning and development specialist in a large corporation. Along with previous experience, he had additional skills that could enhance his position, if he was allowed to use them. He was given an assignment to create a presentation for the annual marketing division meeting, to which his department was reporting.

Being highly creative, Garrett decided to put together a video presentation instead of the usual twenty-minute slide presentation.

The Ego's Response

Garrett works on the video without seeking approval from his manager, Justin. Justin drops by Garrett's desk to check on him, as he often does, creating a feeling of uneasiness and distrust.

Justin: Hi, Garrett. What are you up to?

Garrett: Just working on the marketing presentation.

Justin: Interesting. That doesn't look like a slideshow.

Garrett: Well, actually, I'm doing a short video. I thought it would be unique and a lot more fun. (Using bad judgment, Garrett starts his project without prior approval from his manager.)

Justin: Who do you think you are? You have no business doing this without running it by me. (Justin's tone is immediately caustic, angry, and reactive.)

Garrett: I thought I'd put something together and surprise you with it. (This choice comes from fear or an ego-based objective.)

Justin: Surprise me? Since when do you behave like that in corporate America? This project is representing the entire department, and you have no business doing something different without my prior approval. Do you hear me? (Justin's comments are angry, threatening, and accusatory.)

Garrett: Yes. Well, what do you want me to do now?

Justin: Scrap it and do as I asked.

Garrett: But I've already put hours of work into this!

Justin: Tough. You'll just have to catch up on the slideshow, and by the way, you will have to do it on your own time. I'm not letting any of your other tasks suffer at the expense of this costly and obstinate choice you have made. (In his anger, Justin steps outside the lines of what is legally allowed in corporate America by demanding that Garrett work on a project outside of working hours. Justin's ego has skewed his sense of right and wrong.)

This conversation was not fruitful. Clearly both parties behaved from the place of ego over heart-based directives. This perpetuates a sense of distrust, animosity, and resentment within the department.

The Heart's Response

Garrett goes to his manager's office and approaches him with the idea.

> **Garrett:** Hey, Justin. Do you have a minute? (Garrett respectfully asks Justin if he has the time for him. This shows regard and thoughtfulness.)

> **Justin:** Sure. What's up? (Justin is open and welcoming.)

> **Garrett:** Before I get started on the marketing team presentation, I wanted to run an idea by you. (Garrett asks for permission. This show Justin that he respects him and wants his guidance and feedback.)

> **Justin:** OK.

> **Garrett:** So you know that in my last job I was in the video business?

> **Justin:** Yes.

> **Garrett:** Well, I don't know if I made this clear to you, but I have done camera work, along with editing. Anyway, I had this really fun idea to produce a video for the meeting. It would be so different from the typical slideshow presentation, and it would also take some of the heat off of the team as presenters. (He lists the advantages to his new idea.)

Justin: Sounds like a possibility. Tell me more. How long would it take to create? How much manpower would it involve? What do you envision as the final product? (Justin shows interest. He then asks specific questions that would steer Garrett in the direction of more practical thinking.)

Garrett: Well, because it's video, I'm not going to lie: it'll take more time and manpower than a basic slideshow. That being said, though, I'm happy to work extra hours on my own time to do the editing. I thought we could create a video that highlights the job that our behind the scenes crew does—the cleaning staff, the kitchen staff, and others who work hard here without getting too much credit. (Garrett feels safe and tells Justin the truth—that it would take more time. His idea is altruistic, and he positions it as such.)

Justin: Sounds interesting, but how do you tie that into marketing? (Justin remains open.)

Garrett: Well, I thought it could start us all into a new mindset, where we honor those who don't usually get noticed for their hard work. We would promote or market them, so to speak. We could create a presentation that highlights all the cogs in the wheel that keep this company on its successful path. We could start a new internal promotional campaign in the newsletter that showcases the work that all employees do—how each of us contributes to the success of the business in our own unique ways. It would create a positive buzz among staff and improve morale! (Garrett clearly states his case, integrating the marketing into staff satisfaction.)

Justin: What would you need from me and from the rest of the team? Because this is a departmentwide initiative, you would need input and buy-in from the whole gang. (Justin remains open and shows his support.)

Garrett: Well, I already mentioned it to team members just as a possibility. I made it clear, though, that we'd still need your blessing. (Garrett walks a fine line here by already having discussed the idea with his coworkers. That was not the optimum choice. However, he is clear to point out that he prefaced discussions with the caveat that he would need Justin's approval.)

Justin: And?

Garrett: The gang was pretty excited. I could have them play various roles.

Justin: It might be fun if you created an old-fashioned sepia effect with the video. Like the silent movies. (Justin remains open and offers his own creative ideas. This encourages Garrett and builds upon his enthusiasm.)

Garrett: That'd be great. Then we could underscore it with music, so the team wouldn't have to act out lines. What a great idea! So does that mean you're game? (Garrett does not assume Justin has approved.)

Justin: Let's have a department meeting on this to hash out the details. If all agree, then sure, why not! (Justin shows good management in suggesting that the entire team meet to discuss the idea.)

Garrett: Awesome!

Justin: I knew that we would eventually use some of the other talents and skills you brought along with you. (Justin compliments Garrett on his creativity and proactive choice. This allows Garrett and his coworkers room to explore innovative and new ideas.)

Garrett: Absolutely! Thanks so much for allowing me to express my creativity. I promise you won't be disappointed. (Garrett expresses appreciation and commits to continued efforts.)

In this scenario, by choosing the "yes" stance of the Good Morning Mind, both Garrett and Justin created a win-win situation. In fact, Garrett's video and concept were such a success that the company started a staff showcase, raising morale in the company. Had the egoic conversation ensued, the company would have lost a highly creative and out-of-the-box opportunity.

The Witness-self's Response

Embodying the witness-self, Justin would have encouraged innovation and creative freedom even more. In fact, noting Garrett's propensity for video production, he might have provided him with other responsibilities that carved a path towards more creative enterprises. If he felt that the company was not a good match for Garrett, he might have even directed him to positions in other companies that were more of a match for his prowess.

Innovative Implementation Ideas

- Write a list of your current worries and fears about your business. Rate each fear on a scale from one to ten. Then coach yourself through the greatest fears (or have a reliable friend do so). Ask "What are you most afraid of?" "Could you survive the worst-case scenario?" "What might you do to alleviate this fear?"

- Make a list of all of the fears, big or small, that you have overcome in your life. Acknowledge yourself for having done so.

- Do an inventory of how often you bypass guiding messages from your intuition because they defy "logic." Next time you get a hit to follow something, make a choice to do so, write it down, and note the outcome.

- Organize a monthly innovation brainstorming session with your staff. Allow staff members to plan the meeting and think of a fun theme. Then, without pressure, encourage play and see what new ideas arise.

Habit 4

REDUCE Reactivity and Nurture Proactivity

Incessant reactivity breeds paranoia, conflict, and a volatile workplace. Proactivity is thoughtful, contemplative, and fruitful.

The more mindful you are, the less reactive you become. Mindfulness allows you to step outside of the drama you are engaging in and see it from a more objective point of view. Although I have touched on the benefits of cultivating mindfulness practices in your business, I will discuss them in greater detail in this chapter.

You have already seen demonstrations of mindfulness at work in the heart-based dialogues that I have shared. When you have cultivated mindfulness, it is easier to remain calm and proactive even in volatile situations. You become aware of subtle energy and how it maneuvers in your life and in the lives of others. You are able to watch the dynamics of conversations in a way that is impartial and neutral.

A Quiet Conversation with the Ego

Recently I was invited to speak on a panel on video production. Originally I was to be the sole speaker, but later I was asked to be a part of the panel. My ego sounded off her alarms. In the past, I would have acted from a place of reactivity. I would have taken a defensive stance in the situation. In my insecurity, I would have made sure that I spoke as much as possible, maintaining a one-up on the other panelists.

From the emotional work that I had done, I had learned that it is not wise to judge the ego, so during the session I simply watched her do her dance in quiet and fascinated observation. In those moments when I wanted to plow into the conversation and make myself heard, I sat back and calmed the ego, as I would a needy child: "It's OK, ego. You don't have to be seen. Trust. Sit back and enjoy the exchange. Speak when you are spoken to, and be present. Sit with the intention, 'How may I serve?' Make that your chief aim."

I watched the ego growl in anxiety again. I would continually quiet it. In the past, it would have taken over, but with my new awareness, I was able to calm it and enjoy the experience.

Once I calmed the ego and became more present, I was able to contribute to the conversation in a more powerful way. Once I let the ego go, I felt more connected to the team. I melded into their energy which was highly palpable and very effective. Several attendees approached me afterwards and thanked me for my input. I do not believe I would have received the same response had I let my ego take over. It would have blocked a lot of good energy and would have broadcast an unappealing neediness. It would have turned audience members off.

Conflict over Contrast Profile

When you are able to harness your impulses toward creating conflict, you experience more harmony in your life. What was once undeniably conflictual becomes more neutral, and you are able to be less emotionally triggered and more level-headed. For each of the questions below, choose the number that most closely aligns with your current situation (1 being "not at all" and 10 being "a great deal").

1. Do you find yourself having a black-and-white (right and wrong) response to most issues you face?
1 — 2 — 3 — 4 — 5 — 6 — 7 — 8 — 9 — 10

2. Are you unable to resolve conflicts when they arise?
1 — 2 — 3 — 4 — 5 — 6 — 7 — 8 — 9 — 10

3. Do you find it difficult to let go of past resentments?
1 — 2 — 3 — 4 — 5 — 6 — 7 — 8 — 9 — 10

4. Would those who work with you describe you as argumentative?
1 — 2 — 3 — 4 — 5 — 6 — 7 — 8 — 9 — 10

5. Are you considered rigid and authoritarian in your ways?

1 — 2 — 3 — 4 — 5 — 6 — 7 — 8 — 9 — 10

6. Do you find it hard to agree to disagree when you reach an impasse with others?

1 — 2 — 3 — 4 — 5 — 6 — 7 — 8 — 9 — 10

7. Are you emphatic about doing things by the book?

1 — 2 — 3 — 4 — 5 — 6 — 7 — 8 — 9 — 10

8. Do your subordinates fear you and find you unapproachable?

1 — 2 — 3 — 4 — 5 — 6 — 7 — 8 — 9 — 10

9. Do you struggle to see both sides of an argument?

1 — 2 — 3 — 4 — 5 — 6 — 7 — 8 — 9 — 10

10. Do you struggle to step outside of conflicts and see them objectively?

1 — 2 — 3 — 4 — 5 — 6 — 7 — 8 — 9 — 10

If you scored between 76 and 100, you struggle quite a bit with conflict. Honor yourself for having the honesty and insight to complete this profile with this new realization. First and foremost, you must be gentle and compassionate with yourself as you find yourself in conflict. Know that any external conflict reflects your internal world. Set a strong intention to become more mindful and follow the practices outlined, and you will find yourself in much calmer waters.

If you scored between 51 and 75, you have done some work to become more mindful, but you still have a great deal more to do. Know that you have already started paving your way towards a path of greater ease and less conflict. Commit to compassion and seek neutral ground. Follow the suggestions outlined and track your progress as you transform conflict into contrast in both your personal and business life.

If you scored between 26 and 50, you have accomplished a fair amount of resolution around conflict. Continue to forge ahead, using the tools in this book. Commit to cultivating the witness-self and try to stop before reacting to situations. Know that through discipline and commitment, the ease of living a more mindful life is possible.

If you scored between 10 and 25, congratulations! You are able to see beyond conflict and assess potentially volatile situations in a neutral and productive manner. Continue on the path you have carved for yourself and support your efforts by implementing the suggestions in this book. Honor yourself for your efforts to become more conscious and connected.

Now that you are more aware of yourself in regard to mindfulness, you are ready to take the next steps towards cultivating the witness. Doing so will open up a new world of greater ease, less effort and improved relationships at home and in business.

Conflict Trigger Situation

While this situation is not set in a work environment, I think it is a powerful example of a foundation that encourages honesty. A couple of months ago, my daughter, Bea, was driving behind me, following me in my car. When I came to a stoplight, I noticed in my rearview mirror that she wasn't applying her brakes. I braced myself, ready to be hit. She smashed into my car.

The Ego's Response

Had the two of us reacted from the fear-based ego, the conversation might have gone something like this:

> **Theresa (getting out of car to explore the damage):** Bea, what the heck were you doing? I watched in my rearview mirror as you smashed into my bumper. Look at it. This is going to cost a fortune to fix! (She attacks and shames Bea and continues to block three lanes of traffic.)

> **Bea:** I'm sorry. You didn't give me enough notice. You forced your brakes at the last minute. (She responds with a counterattack.)

> **Theresa:** I did not. You weren't watching! I can't believe you hit me!

The conversation would have continued in attack and counterattack. Ultimately it would have affected their relationship in a detrimental way.

The Heart's Response

Fortunately, we were both able to respond to the incident from our hearts. Here is how the conversation transpired:

> **Bea (as they both get out of their cars and examine the damage):** Sorry, mom. I can't believe I hit you!

> **Theresa:** That's OK, honey. Let's head back home to avoid blocking traffic.

> **Bea (upon arrival):** Mom, I don't know what happened. There must be something wrong with my brakes. I tried to hit them, but they didn't work. (She responds by defending her actions.)

> **Theresa (listening without malice or judgment):** Why don't you drive the car around the block to further test the brakes? (She shows that she hears Bea and wants to investigate further.)

> **Bea (returning after driving the car around the block):** Now I remember. It wasn't the brakes. It was my fault. I was being aggressive. I was concerned that another car was going to get in front of me, and I was driving faster than I should have. When it was time to hit the brakes, I couldn't hit them fast enough. I was wrong, and I'm so sorry. (Because she was not attacked for her error, she owned up to it, and we all left the situation a little bit more conscious.)

Theresa: That's OK, sweetie. I'm just glad you hit my car over someone else's. And I'm so proud of you for being so honest, honey!

Bea: Well, you always taught me that that honesty and trust are really important, that if I was honest with you, I would never be punished.

Theresa: Awesome! (While I can list the myriad of mistakes I have made as a parent, in this case I felt a twinge of pride.)

The Witness-self's Response

From the witness's perspective, the incident would not have been perceived as an accident. It would have been seen as a situation that helped to raise the consciousness and the connection between the two individuals involved.

To take this scenario to the workplace, is your working environment open, honest, and forgiving, or hard, cold, and attacking? If the environment does not encourage openness and honesty, what might you do to encourage it? It can start with you. In whatever position you hold, you can commit to your own inner journey of transformation. As you continue to practice honesty, integrity, and the Good Morning Mind techniques, you will become less reactive and more proactive. Be patient with yourself. It won't necessarily happen overnight, but know that with commitment and a strong intention, positive change is possible.

Build a Culture of Encouragement

When there is conflict in a work environment, staff are running on fight-or-flight mode. It kicks their adrenal system into high gear, and they eventually burn out. This atmosphere is also combative, insinuating that some are right while others are wrong. It is toxic and needs to be repaired.

One of the first steps towards reparation is building upon a foundation of honesty. When people feel safe enough to be honest, they will start sharing in a way that unites instead of divides.

Mindfulness Scan Meditation

Find a comfortable spot where you will not be disturbed. Ideally you should be in a seated position with your spine erect. Turn off your cell phone and any other potential distractions. Take a few deep breaths in. As you inhale, see your body filling with clean, fresh air. As you exhale, release any heaviness, anxieties, or frustrations. Now, on your next three inhalations, tighten up all of your muscles. Tighten them as much as you can. As you exhale, release the muscles. Then allow your attention to go to your breath. Watch it entering and exiting just below your nostrils for a couple of breaths.

Now, starting with the top of your head, start to scan your body. Just observe and feel into every part of it. Don't try to make any changes. If, for example, you notice tension, just witness it, sit with it, and move on. Continue to scan your body, allowing yourself to be present with each body part. Observing and not judging. Simply be present.

Once you have scanned your body, do the "yes" process. See your heart filling with white light, and see that light radiate outward to every cell in your body. Then see that light radiate beyond your body to all of your colleagues, friends, and family members. See it igniting the hearts of everyone in the world.

To end the meditation, contemplate all that you are grateful for in your life. When you feel ready, open your eyes.

Encouraging introspection and proactivity will build a trusting and conscious work environment. Next time you react, see if you can catch yourself in the act. If you can, you might just call it out for what it is: "I'm sorry. I was reactive. I was triggered in that moment. Upon reflection, I see that . . ." When you commit to honesty and own your shortcomings, they will not remain as shortcomings. They will change from liabilities into possibilities.

Habit 5

ENCOURAGE Community over Competitiveness

Building relationships on generosity trumps previous negative patterns and practices. If your business has been based on the old win-lose competitive paradigm, you can shift it by creating a system that activates and incentivizes cooperation and supports workplace community.

Although competitiveness can breed contempt, it is one of the most difficult attitudes in the workplace to release. However, when an organization models and recognizes generosity of spirit from the top down, it can create a work environment that thrives on cooperation and team spirit.

Competitiveness Profile

While many consider competitiveness to be fun and friendly, it can often lead to anger and toxic interactions. With competition, there are winners and losers. Creating an environment of cooperation over competitiveness builds a much stronger, more cohesive community within your business. Take a few minutes to learn more about how competitive you are (or are not). For each of the questions below, choose the number that most closely aligns with your current situation (1 being "not at all" and 10 being "a great deal").

1. Do you get angry when you lose at a competition?

1 — 2 — 3 — 4 — 5 — 6 — 7 — 8 — 9 — 10

2. Do you find competition to be stressful instead of fun?

1 — 2 — 3 — 4 — 5 — 6 — 7 — 8 — 9 — 10

3. Do you compete with others even when you are not in a competitive situation?

1 — 2 — 3 — 4 — 5 — 6 — 7 — 8 — 9 — 10

4. Do you get angry or impatient when competing?

1 — 2 — 3 — 4 — 5 — 6 — 7 — 8 — 9 — 10

5. When the contest is in question, do you struggle to acquiesce and allow your opponent to win?

1 — 2 — 3 — 4 — 5 — 6 — 7 — 8 — 9 — 10

6. Do you prefer competitive activities over leisurely ones?

1 — 2 — 3 — 4 — 5 — 6 — 7 — 8 — 9 — 10

7. Are you considered a poor loser?

1 — 2 — 3 — 4 — 5 — 6 — 7 — 8 — 9 — 10

8. Do others see you as a leader rather than a team player?

1 — 2 — 3 — 4 — 5 — 6 — 7 — 8 — 9 — 10

9. Are you a gracious winner?

1 — 2 — 3 — 4 — 5 — 6 — 7 — 8 — 9 — 10

10. Do you view your business ventures as competitive rather than cooperative?

1 — 2 — 3 — 4 — 5 — 6 — 7 — 8 — 9 — 10

If you scored between 76 and 100, you may be too competitive for your own good. Evaluate how much your competitive nature is interfering with your life. You may wish to shift your focus toward building cooperative relationships rather than winning competitions. Doing so may decrease stress and create the intimacy in your life that you may be lacking.

If you scored between 51 and 75, although you are not completely in competition mode, you are quite competitive in nature. Reflect on what your competitiveness is taking away from your life experiences. Play with the possibility of allowing others to win. When losing triggers a negative reaction, have a compassionate dialogue with the part of yourself that is struggling.

If you scored between 26 and 50, you are somewhat competitive, although competitiveness does not rule your life. Continue to cultivate cooperation and connection in your relationships. As you do, you will find competition less important than it may currently be in your life.

If you scored between 10 and 25, congratulations! You have found balance between the cooperative and competitive aspects of your personality. While you may enjoy competition, it is not a driving force in your life. Continue in the direction you are going, knowing that you are on the right track.

Now that you have a better sense of your attitude toward competition, you can develop greater balance between your competitive and cooperative natures. Competition is not bad in itself, but overcompetitive-ness can wreak havoc on your relationships both at work and at home.

Generosity of Spirit

When generosity of spirit is cultivated in the workplace as opposed to competitiveness, the staff develops more pride and self-respect. Egos are quelled, and altruism kicks in.

I was recently sharing my career path with two dear friends and fellow Toastmasters, Larry New and Stella Lorens. They are both highly successful lead-ers and very well-regarded in their businesses. When I mentioned that my next step in the evolution of my company, Edu-Tainment Productions, would be shar-ing the wisdom of my two most recent books through keynote speaking, Larry said he had a friend with whom he was planning on pitching a keynote concept. He said that he would hook the two of us up and that he was sure the gentleman would be interested in hiring me to do a keynote within the next couple of months.

I was shocked. "What about you, Larry?" I said. "Wouldn't I be competition for you?"

His response overwhelmed me: "If you get the gig, I'm not yet ready for it."

Stella went on to list a variety of her industry connections to help promote my books. Both of them were selfless, generous, and thoughtful in their initiatives to assist me.

Had Larry been responding from the level of the ego, he would have seen me as competition and done everything he could to keep me from succeeding. He would not have shared this connection with me. But he responded from the heart and from a place of abundance. He had surrendered to the fact that if he did not get the speaking engagement, he wasn't ready for it.

This was a powerful lesson in generosity of spirit that I deeply appreciated. Both Stella and Larry modeled cooperation over competition in an exemplary way.

Marianne Williamson's Compassionate Cooperation

One author I really enjoyed producing for at Nightingale-Conant Corporation was Marianne Williamson. Above and beyond being a top-notch inspirational speaker, she is authentic, transparent, and brutally honest about her own issues. I continue to have the utmost respect for her.

In 2019 Marianne became a Democratic presidential candidate. While the competition was fierce, she did something unheard of. She invited Andrew Yang, one of her rivals, to be interviewed by her. During the interview, she praised him for his policies and platform and was incredibly generous and gracious. In the social media comments that followed the interview, many said they would vote for Andrew.

Marianne was willing to put her own agenda aside to support the competition. With all of the unrest, greed, and self-serving attacks in politics, it was rare and refreshing to see someone put aside competition in favor of cooperation.

I also learned that Marianne will speak for a minimal fee compared to her contemporaries. In addition, she has a policy of allowing all to attend her presentations regardless of whether they can pay. She is clearly committed to being accessible and prioritizes getting her message heard over profit.

In fact, during one Empowering Women seminar I attended in Los Angeles several years ago, Marianne discovered that a woman who was to share hotel costs with me decided not to attend, leaving me high and dry (she wanted me to use my connection with Marianne to acquire a singing position at the event, and I would not comply). Marianne found out about the situation and actually gave me a free room at the hotel. She has my utmost respect, not only as a wise and inspiring metaphysical teacher, but as an individual with high ethics and integrity. Her generous and inspiring spirit is deeply appreciated. She embodies the grace that comes from choosing cooperation over competitiveness and love over fear. It's no accident that she titled one of the two programs we recorded *Everyday Grace!*

Innovative Implementation Ideas

- This is an enjoyable team-building exercise that I used to do with staff during training sessions. Lay out small tarps around the room and have groups of staff stand on each tarp. Then explain that the tarp they are on is a raft. They are in a lagoon, surrounded by crocodiles. As a team, they have to find a way to turn the raft around without touching the floor (so that the side touching the floor is right side up). Anyone who falls into the lagoon will be eaten by the crocodiles. The team that flips their raft first wins. This is a wonderful exercise in building team spirit, and it is also very eye-opening. On one occasion, I remember one staff member bullying the rest. They followed her horrible directives and failed miserably at the task. No one was willing to cross her, and they all suffered for it. On the other hand, I've seen staff work together and strategize in a cohesive and effective way. You can learn a great deal about your staff simply by having them do this exercise.

- Practice the "How may I serve?" principle. There is a very distinct chain of command in the world of business. First and foremost is the customer, then the staff, who serves the customers, and then the management, who serves the staff. In whatever role you play in the business, ask your coworkers, customers, or others, "How may I better serve you?" Note their response, and find steps you can take to better serve them. Then note how you feel about yourself after doing so.

- Create a "How may I better serve you?" tracking initiative in your workplace that encourages top-notch service among your team.

- Hold a workshop in active listening skills for your staff. Teach them how to be present when others speak. You can do the telephone game as an opener. (They form a circle, and someone says a basic sentence. It is whispered from person to person in the circle until complete.) Most often the final sentence does not in any way resemble the original one.

- In the Story Chain Gang game, each person in a circle goes in order through the alphabet from A to Z. They listen to the previous word spoken and add another word from the next letter of the alphabet. In this end they come up with a story, often a nonsensical one.

- Have staff get into groups of two. Then provide them with a volatile work scenario. Ask them to role-play, first from an ego-based fear response, and then again from the heart-based response. Have them share any "aha" moments or insights they receive in exploring the two different ways to respond.

Habit 6

SHIFT from Selfishness to Self-fullness

Labeling someone as selfish is shaming. Encouraging conscious selfishness (self-fullness) fosters self-care and fosters peace and well-being among staff.

When staff truly care for themselves, they will be healthier and happier. Consequently, care for your business and your clients will naturally and organically follow.

We've Got It Wrong

Most of us have been raised on the moral principle that we should put others before ourselves. Since early childhood, this has often been drilled into us by culture, religion, and family.

I encourage you to consider that perhaps we have it all wrong. We are backwards in our selflessness, and that is why it does not work. We have been exposed to powerful messages that may be in error. One is the Golden Rule: "Do unto others as you would have them do unto you." Many have interpreted this commandment to mean that we need to stop being selfish; we need to become more altruistic and love others first.

I, however, contend that we have the commandment backwards. In order to give to others, we have to first take care of ourselves. If we do not, we are giving from a place of "should" rather than from a natural, organic progression in which our own needs are taken care of, so the desire to support others comes from an authentic desire to serve. Then and only then can we care for others with a full heart and an honest disposition.

We perpetuate self-shaming in many aspects of our lives. Whether in business or family interactions, people often give prematurely, sometimes because of peer pressures. They focus on caring for others before they have taken care of their own needs. When this is the case, giving is often rooted in resentment, bitterness, depletion, shame, and self-neglect.

If, however, we were each to first take care of our own needs, we would feel energized, satiated, and ready to give. We would do so from a naturally altruistic state. We would be filled, and we would be ready to fill others.

Conscious Selfishness in Management

Let's take this premise to the world of business. If, as a business owner or manager, you are constantly taking care of everyone but yourself, in a very short time you will find yourself exhausted. This in turn will affect your temperament, the quality of your work, and your energetic imprint on the business. If, however, you take care of your needs first and foremost, you are energized. You feel good. You feel complete, so you have the stamina and the emotional wherewithal to support your staff and your business in a much more potent way.

Supporting Staff to Grow beyond You

Have you heard of those rare businesses where management actually coach their staff to move beyond their current position to a better position in another company? While this is rare, it does occur. At first glance, one would think that there would be no benefits in such an altruistic stance; it would only hinder the business. But consider the reputation you would gain among potential staff members and within the industry. Word would get around, and before you know it, you'd have a lineup of quality potential employees who want to do their best for your company *and* themselves.

Look at this paradigm from the perspective of your staff. If you push them, they struggle with burnout, resentment, and job dissatisfaction. Imagine yourself as one of your staff. Your manager welcomes you each day. Not only do they create a joyful and harmonious work environment, but they also coach you on pursuing your deepest goals and desires. How would you feel about going into work? How loyal would you be to that boss and that business? How highly would you speak about the business to friends, family, clients, and others? Your business would be associated with goodness, and your staff would appreciate it and reflect it back to you twofold.

When you care for your customers because you are cared for, there is no leap. You are modeling the commitment to serve that was modeled to you.

Viewing this shift from the perspective of supporting customers, at first glance one might assume that a self-full employee would not entirely care for the customer. The employee would not tolerate any verbal abuse and would do whatever it takes to protect himself from an angry customer. But if the employee has cultivated the habits outlined in this book, including self-accountability and compassion, this will not be the case.

Conscious Selfishness Profile

While many consider selfishness a trait that should be scorned and discouraged, if you dig deeper, you will find that true selfishness that is not based in fear but in self-care serves the individual and those with whom they are working. Take a few minutes to learn more about how consciously selfish you are (or are not). For each of the questions below, choose the number that most closely aligns with your current situation (1 being "not at all" and 10 being "a great deal").

1. Do you consider yourself extremely giving, almost to a fault?

1 — 2 — 3 — 4 — 5 — 6 — 7 — 8 — 9 — 10

2. Do you usually find yourself too exhausted to follow through on the self-care you desire?

1 — 2 — 3 — 4 — 5 — 6 — 7 — 8 — 9 — 10

3. Were you raised with the belief that you should love your neighbor before yourself?

1 — 2 — 3 — 4 — 5 — 6 — 7 — 8 — 9 — 10

4. Do you wish you could give yourself more "me" time throughout your day?

1 — 2 — 3 — 4 — 5 — 6 — 7 — 8 — 9 — 10

5. Do you wish you had more time to eat right and exercise?

1 — 2 — 3 — 4 — 5 — 6 — 7 — 8 — 9 — 10

6. Do you always put the needs of your family first?

1 — 2 — 3 — 4 — 5 — 6 — 7 — 8 — 9 — 10

7. Do people call you "saintly" for all of the giving you do?

1 — 2 — 3 — 4 — 5 — 6 — 7 — 8 — 9 — 10

8. Are you overinvolved in volunteer work?

1 — 2 — 3 — 4 — 5 — 6 — 7 — 8 — 9 — 10

9. Do you struggle to delegate tasks to others when overwhelmed?

1 — 2 — 3 — 4 — 5 — 6 — 7 — 8 — 9 — 10

10. Do you wish there were more hours in the day so that you can have more free, fun time in your life?

1 — 2 — 3 — 4 — 5 — 6 — 7 — 8 — 9 — 10

If you scored between 76 and 100, you may be too selfless for your own good. While giving to others is an honorable trait, doing so to your own detriment can be toxic for both parties. Each day make an effort to shift your attention to your own self-care. You can start by taking tiny steps. Taking only five minutes each day to stop and relax will start to make a difference. In time, you will find that as your energy grows, you are able to give from a place of energetic fullness as opposed to depletion.

If you scored between 51 and 75, although you are not overwhelmed by complete selflessness, you struggle to put yourself first. Reflect on the ways in which you sacrifice yourself for others and list them on a piece of paper. Then go through the list and see if there are any tasks you can take off the list. Setting the intention is the first step towards greater energy through self-care.

If you scored between 26 and 50, you have made some strides in self-care, although you still have some work to do (or not to do!). As you give yourself permission to love, honor, and nurture yourself, you will find that others will react accordingly. You are a wonderful human being. You don't have to be "doing" to be lovable.

If you scored between 10 and 25, congratulations! You are stellar at self-care. You are doing a wonderful job at placing your well-being first and foremost on your priority list. You likely find that you have more energy to give to others because you make self-care a priority in life. Continue in the direction you are going, knowing that you are on the right track.

Now that you have a better sense of how consciously selfish you are, you can work towards more self-honoring and greater self-care. You will note that the more you care for yourself, the less resentful you are towards others. When you give from a place of energized enthusiasm, you are truly giving from your expanded heart.

Conscious Selfishness Trigger Situation

Ben works at a condominium complex. He handles a myriad of customers. Mr. Motley has visited the management office daily for the past week. He has been constantly complaining about the temperature of the pool, and he has started to berate Ben.

The Ego's Response

Mr. Motley: What is wrong with you people? I don't know how many times I've come in here, and you don't do a damned thing. I checked out the pool again this morning, and it is too danged cold. I'm not some spring chicken, you know. This is a senior living complex. We can't take the cold water. What are you trying to do—give us heart attacks or something?

Ben: Mr. Motley, I've told you that there is nothing I can do.

Mr. Motley: Well, I'm not happy with that. You young ones—wait until you are my age and have arthritis. Then you'll see!

Ben: Well, Mr. Motley, what can I say? That'll be a long time coming. (Mr. Motley leaves angry and dissatisfied.)

The Heart's Response

Susan is highly satisfied with her position as the complex manager. She has "selfishly" taken care of her basic needs. She always takes her lunch and other breaks and insists that her staff do the same. She takes time out in her day to meditate. When overwhelmed, she'll step out of the office and take a walk or a two-minute dance break. She feels calm and is committed to responding to situations with an open heart. She supports her staff in doing the same. She has given Ben time and space to find his own solutions to Mr. Motley and his complaint. In time, she decides to step in and model the way in which Ben can open-heartedly respond to Mr. Motley.

Susan: Hello, Mr. Motley. How are you today? I love your bathing suit. Luminous green. That color really uplifts me on dreary days like today!

Mr. Motley: Yah, well, thanks. Now where's that boy? I've been in here I don't know how many times the past several weeks, and the kid is useless. You ought to find someone older, someone who understands. Anyway, what the heck is up with that pool?

Susan: I hear your frustration, Mr. Motley. Ben is a wonderful young man, and he is a dedicated worker. I am lucky to have him here. I'm sorry that you feel frustrated. Please rest assured that Ben and I are working together to provide the best possible experience for you here at Evergreen Park Condominiums. As far as the pool is concerned, I understand your frustrations. I myself do not like cold-water pools. In fact I like them to be about the temperature of a relaxing hot bath.

Mr. Motley: Exactly! So what gives? Are you gonna fix it?

Susan: Actually, Mr. Motley, the truth is that it is an outdoor pool. During the wintertime, even when we have the thermostat up as high as we can get it, It can only reach certain temperatures because of the cold air around it. But I've been thinking about your problem, and I think I've found a solution. There is a wonderful hot tub at the other side of the complex.

Mr. Motley: The other side of the complex? You want to give me a heart attack! I don't have the stamina to get to the other side of the complex every time I want a relaxing swim!

Susan: Of course not, Mr. Motley. As you know, we have a couple of courtesy shuttles here at the complex. We'd be happy to drive you over to the tub whenever you feel like a dip. You can either give us a call each day when you are ready to head over, or if you'd prefer, we can schedule a daily pickup time for you. Which would you prefer?

Mr. Motley: Well . . . I don't know. I'd rather call you when I'm ready, but am I gonna have to wait long?

Susan: No, Mr. Motley. We have several shuttles on hand. We appreciate your patronage and look forward to making your life as relaxing as possible.

Mr. Motley: Well, now that's what I call service. Thank you, Susan!

Susan: Thank you, Mr. Motley.

In this case, Mr. Motley's frustration was remedied with a creative option that Susan came up with during her meditation. She often found that when she took the time to sit back and quiet her mind, solutions to situations would often reveal themselves, as was the case here.

Susan would then take Ben aside and ask him about what he witnessed between her and Mr. Motley. She would then do a couple of role plays in which she would approach Ben as the angry, closed-hearted customer, encouraging him to remain openhearted in his response. He could then experience for himself how maintaining an open heart and holding yourself accountable for your customers' well-being defuses negative energy and rectifies the situation.

The Witness-self's Response

If Susan had responded to the situation from her witness-self, in her mind's eye, there would be no problem that was unmanageable. She would respond to Mr. Motley with deep compassion and appreciation. Being consciously selfish and committed to her own growth, she would feel energized and ready to handle any situation that was brought her way. Being preactive, she would have already had the shuttle ready and be waiting to take Mr. Motley to the hot tub. Without knowing why, he would have left the exchange uplifted and energized. (When one is immersed in the energy of awakened individuals, one's energy is raised whether one is aware of it or not.)

Organic Loyalty

*False loyalty that is forced upon staff is based on
a temporary state of servitude. Organic loyalty
comes from within and encourages permanence.*

Organic loyalty is not forced upon staff. It is deliberate and occurs naturally when they feel supported, nurtured, and cared for. When you create a work environment that is joyful and you encourage staff to take good care of themselves, they naturally fall in love with you and your organization. They enjoy their jobs and look forward to the workday ahead.

Organic Loyalty Trigger Situation

After graduating from college, Edward supplemented his income by doing temporary office work. While he sought permanent full-time work, he thought that along with paying the bills, doing temporary work would expose him to a variety of work environments. Within a couple of months of working as the executive assistant to Amanda, the CEO of a government organization, Edward was offered a freelance position that would pay a great deal more.

The Ego's Response

Had Edward responded to the situation from his egoic mind, he might not have adequately informed Amanda of the new position. He might have immediately called in sick and eventually lied about the position offered to him. Worse yet, fearing confrontation, he may have simply not shown up, leaving her without a replacement. Amanda might have contacted Edward, and the following conversation might have transpired.

Edward: Hello.

Amanda: Edward? This is Amanda. Where have you been? (Amanda starts the conversation in an angry and reactive stance.)

Edward: Umm, I haven't been well. (Edward feels defensive and lies.)

Amanda: Why didn't you call and let me know? I've been stuck without any replacement staff to support me. This is a crazy time of year, and loads of work have been piling up. (Amanda continues to attack.)

Edward: Sorry.

Amanda: When will you be back?

Edward: Actually, I won't be coming back. (Edward avoids telling the truth until pressured by Amanda.)

Amanda: Why not? Why didn't you give me some kind of warning? (Amanda continues with an angry, attacking tone of voice.)

Edward: I don't know. I never thought about it. (Edward's response is apathetic and insensitive.)

Amanda: You never thought about it? What is going on?

Edward: Actually, I've been offered a new job, and it pays much more than you do. I'm going to take it. (Edward shares the news and in his defensive, reactive state, he attacks Amanda by criticizing the pay he receives.)

Amanda: So much for integrity and loyalty. (Amanda further attacks.)

Edward: Working for you has not been easy, you know. Onward and upward. (Edward uses sarcasm to end the conversation.)

Amanda: Thanks a lot! (She ends the exchange on a sour note, using sarcasm to further attack Edward.)

The Heart's Response

If, however, Edward approached Amanda and told the truth with an open heart, and if Amanda responded from her heart as well, the conversation might be more like this:

Edward: Amanda, do you have a minute? I've got something to tell you. (Edward opens the conversation with a respectful and warm tone.)

Amanda: Sure. What's up? (Amanda responds in a welcoming way.)

Edward: Well, I'm kind of nervous. (Edward is transparent about his feelings. In his honesty, he is showing his vulnerability.)

Amanda: No need for the nerves. What's up? (Amanda continues to be warm and encouraging.)

Edward: While I've really enjoyed working with you, I've been offered a new job, and I want to take it. (Edward opens the statement with a compliment and proceeds to tell the truth.)

Amanda: Really? Tell me more. (Amanda shows interest and remains open and nonreactive.)

Edward: It's a freelance job at XYZ company, and the position is related to the field that I think I want to pursue for my future career.

Amanda: Wonderful! Congratulations, Edward. While I'll miss you and the great work that you do, I'm happy for you. (Amanda responds in a supportive and positive manner.)

Edward: You're not angry?

Amanda: No, not at all. While disappointed, I am grateful for the work that you've done over the past several months. If something better comes your way, you have to take it! I'd do the same. (Amanda honestly shares her disappointment, but expresses empathy and gratitude towards Edward.)

Edward: Wow! Thank you for being so understanding. I've informed the new employer that I'll need to give you at least two weeks' notice prior to leaving. And if you can't find a replacement within the two weeks, I'd be happy to come in on weekends to help out. Would that work for you? (Edward has cultivated an organic loyalty towards Amanda. He is moved by her understanding and appreciation. In response, he is ready to go the extra mile and work weekends to support her. He then shows he is respectful of Amanda by checking in to see if his plan works for her.)

Amanda: Absolutely, Ed. Again, congratulations and thanks for all of the hard work that you've done the past several months. You can always count on me for references in the future. (The conversation ends on a positive and mutually supportive note.)

The Witness-self's Response

If one or both parties were awakened, there would be an even greater sense of ease and effortlessness to the conversation. Each would be comfortable to ask for what they want and respond in a way that was even more open, supportive, and compassionate.

Innovative Implementation Ideas

- Have a productive procrastination day when staff can clean out their desks, go through closets, or do other things that they have been avoiding. Make it a fun day and encourage joyful interaction among staff.

- Model, create, and sustain authentic and heartfelt internal and external customer care. Catch staff treating customers well. Have a customer feedback box and encourage customers to write about their experiences with your staff. Showcase their efforts with a staff recognition board.

- Create a self-full board on which staff can note the times that they took proper care of themselves. Commend them for doing so.

- Encourage staff to take a couple of two- to three-minute "me" breaks during their day. Have them watch a funny three-minute funny video or a music video that energizes and inspires them. Perhaps you could create two daily team "me" breaks, like laughter yoga or a three-minute disco dance-a-thon.

Habit 7

EMBRACE Diversity in the Workplace

It takes all kinds of people to make this world a fascinating and magical place. Choose to celebrate yourself and everyone else who contributes to your business, big or small. Honor differences—in fact, celebrate them and do so fully and generously. Without contrast, you can get lost in the mundane and flat world of sameness.

Now more than ever, there is an awakening of the masses. We are reaching a tipping point, when prejudice is no longer tolerated by humankind. Although there is an opening towards greater acceptance of all, there is a counterculture that supports the closing of hearts and minds—an intolerance that is fighting against compassion, universal acceptance, and inclusivity. The more I have delved into my own inner integrity, the more my prejudices have revealed themselves to me. Many were surprising and even troubling.

I believe that ignorance and prejudice are most often learned behaviors. That being said, being brought up in a prejudiced and closed-minded environment does not give you carte blanche to remain there. Facing your prejudices squarely and directly takes great self-honesty and courage. Observing and shifting your own personal prejudices can be a catalyst towards courageous (and contagious) changes in the workplace.

While we are all aware of the need for diversity in culture, religion, and sexual orientation, we may be less educated about the importance of emotional diversity. As awareness of mental illness becomes more prevalent, it is imperative to educate ourselves on how to support those who are suffering from it. Very often learning starts within ourselves. We need to reflect on, process, and shift our own preconceived notions about mental illness before we can experience mass healing.

Emotional turmoil is a part of the human condition. Our lives are filled with emotional roller coasters that take us from fear to love and everywhere in between. Very often the thing that drives us to our knees is ultimately the catalyst toward deeper self-appreciation and self-acceptance. The more we understand that mental illness is, in fact, illness (like any physical condition), the more we can let go of labels and biases that reek of judgment and misunderstandings.

In this chapter, I will touch on a myriad of mental illnesses, specifically anxiety and personality disorders (PDs) that you might encounter among family members, friends, or in the workplace. Becoming informed about how to respond to these disorders in an open, compassionate, and heart-based manner will create a more conscious and supportive environment for all.

To start, take the following Emotional Self-awareness Profile. It will provide you with a mirror that will reflect your emotional awareness (or lack thereof) back at you. This will support you in breaking through your prejudices so you can live a life free of preconceptions and filled with deeper understanding and greater heart-based connection.

Emotional Self-awareness Profile

Complete this profile to better understand your own emotional state—what circumstances trigger you the most and how you respond to them. For each question below, choose the number that most closely aligns with your current state (1 being "not at all" and 10 being "a great deal").

1. Are you extremely self-aware (aware of what you think and feel and why you do so)?

1 — 2 — 3 — 4 — 5 — 6 — 7 — 8 — 9 — 10

2. Have you gone through therapy, retreats, or other vehicles that support your greater self-awareness?

1 — 2 — 3 — 4 — 5 — 6 — 7 — 8 — 9 — 10

3. Do you feel compassionate towards others as they struggle with their own emotional challenges?

1 — 2 — 3 — 4 — 5 — 6 — 7 — 8 — 9 — 10

4. Do others come to you for advice on emotional issues?

1 — 2 — 3 — 4 — 5 — 6 — 7 — 8 — 9 — 10

5. Do you welcome feedback from others when you've gone off course?

1 — 2 — 3 — 4 — 5 — 6 — 7 — 8 — 9 — 10

6. Would others consider you an expert at relationship building?

1 — 2 — 3 — 4 — 5 — 6 — 7 — 8 — 9 — 10

7. Are you courageous in facing your inner demons?

1 — 2 — 3 — 4 — 5 — 6 — 7 — 8 — 9 — 10

8. Are you able to witness the emotional pain of others without feeling compelled to rescue them?

1 — 2 — 3 — 4 — 5 — 6 — 7 — 8 — 9 — 10

9. Are you committed to continuous self-exploration?

1 — 2 — 3 — 4 — 5 — 6 — 7 — 8 — 9 — 10

10. Do you believe in your own intrinsic goodness?

1 — 2 — 3 — 4 — 5 — 6 — 7 — 8 — 9 — 10

If you scored between 76 and 100, congratulations! You are extremely self-aware and are comfortable in your own shoes. While you may struggle with anxiety or stress, you are open to discovering tools and techniques that can help you weather life's occasional storms. Continue to explore yourself on your journey towards greater awareness and consciousness. You will know that you have come far when you note a challenge as it arises, recognize the root of that challenge without having to revisit its source, feel compassion towards yourself, and trust that you already have the knowledge and insight required to heal it (and if you don't, you are willing to seek guidance from an expert).

If you scored between 51 and 75, you have already done a significant amount of work towards healing old wounds and becoming more self-aware. Continue your self-exploration, knowing that challenges will arise. Do not hesitate to seek professional guidance should you find yourself stuck in a cycle of dysfunctional feelings or behaviors. Have compassion for yourself and others, noting that if you could have done better at that time, you would have.

If you scored between 26 and 50, you have done some work on exploring your inner world, and it would be of great value for you to continue to do so. While many believe that reaching out to experts for assistance is a sign of weakness, the opposite is true. It takes great courage and wisdom to ask for help. Know that emotional struggles are part of the human condition, and do not judge yourself when you respond to situations in overreactive ways. Admitting your apparent errors is the first step towards healing them. Know that you can move beyond them. It takes courage, determination, and the commitment to do so. Above all else, strive to be as compassionate as you can with yourself.

If you scored between 10 and 25, honor yourself for being honest when doing this profile. While there is a great deal that you can learn about human dynamics and your own emotional healing, the fact that you are reading this book and responding to the questions with integrity is a sign that you are on the right track. Before taking any steps, be kind to yourself and see yourself as you would a struggling child. Forgive yourself for your mistakes, and begin to look at your perceived shortcomings with curiosity and a commitment to deeper understanding. It would be fruitful to seek guidance from an accredited therapist or self-empowerment program to gain greater clarity. They can provide you with tools and techniques to support you on your self-awareness journey.

Taboos against Mental Illness
In this section, I would like to share some suggestions on healing a toxic workplace by using heart-based interactions. I will focus on fifteen of the most prominent personality and anxiety disorders. I do not claim to be an expert on these disorders, and I am in no way

trying to trivialize them or claim that there are simple, magical remedies to these complex conditions. However, from my own research and self-exploration, I hope I can offer perspectives that you may not have previously considered. Let the following pages serve as guidelines rather than definitive how-tos. If this segment awakens your curiosity, I encourage you to explore further and deeper.

Not too long ago, there was a real stigma associated with mental illness. Talk of mental disturbances of any kind was often hushed in the home and silenced in the workplace. When I graduated from university in 1985, I got a job at IBM. At that time, it was taboo to reveal that I was seeing a therapist. I told no one.

That being said, I was also an actress, and in the world of theater, therapy and self-exploration were the norm. In fact, they were expected and openly discussed among fellow actors. After all, how could you effectively portray a complex character when you are not privy to their emotional make-up—or to your own? As actors, we had to be able to access a myriad of emotional states if we wanted to portray our characters with unabashed expression and authenticity.

Thank Goddess for acting! I was compelled to investigate my own mental challenges from my late teens on, and that curiosity has been the catalyst to a much richer and more fulfilling life. Self-exploration has provided the foundation upon which I can assess the prejudices and belief systems that I have accumulated throughout my life. The more I have explored the world within me, the safer I have felt to explore the outer world. I traveled extensively throughout the world, very often curious and alone. I don't believe that I would have had the courage to do so without addressing the emotional issues that could have made my inner world feel like an unsafe place.

Personality Disorders

Before we go any further, I want to clarify what a personality disorder is. Personality disorders are mental illnesses that are deeply ingrained and are characterized as maladaptive patterns of behavior of a specific kind. They typically manifest by adolescence and cause long-term difficulties in personal relationships and in social functioning. Without treatment, these conditions usually become inflexible and long-lasting. Personality disorder patterns are evident in at least two of these areas: (1) the way in which one thinks about oneself and others; (2) the way in which one responds emotionally to situations; (3) the way in which one relates to others; or (4) the way in which one controls one's behaviors. We are going to focus on ten types of personality disorders: antisocial, avoidant, bipolar, borderline, dependent, histrionic, narcissistic, paranoid, passive-aggressive, and schizoid.

Anxieties

The National Institute of Mental Health defines anxiety disorders as "anxiety that does not go away and can worsen over time." While occasional anxiety due to additional stressors is an expected part of life, when symptoms interfere with daily activities such as schoolwork, job performance and relationships, it becomes a disorder of concern. We are going to focus on five types of anxiety disorders: generalized, obsessive-compulsive, panic, posttraumatic stress, and social phobia.

The Effects of Personality and Anxiety Disorders in the Workplace

While it is the human condition to have idiosyncrasies and unusual behavior traits, a certifiable personality or anxiety disorder can adversely affect the workplace in the following ways. It can:

- Create intense and dramatic situations that can leave staff stressed and on edge.

- Create a feeling of ungrounded uneasiness in the work environment.

- Cost the company financially through litigation costs and financial compensation for both the victim and the perpetrator (often mentally ill perpetrators do not recognize their role in the dysfunction).

- Affect the quality and productivity of the workplace. Abuse of power can take many forms, from slowing production to sexual harassment.

- Create distrust among staff, as some mentally ill individuals may do things like taking credit for the work of others.

- Impede healthy relationships, creating challenges that can affect productivity as energy, time, and effort are being spent on avoiding workplace drama.

- Create a danger zone. In extreme cases, violent acts such as homicide, battery, rape, computer sabotage, and email harassment can occur in the workplace.

On the other hand, addressing anxieties and disorders in a healthy and informed way can deepen relationships and build a solid foundation at your workplace. They can be the vehicle by which staff members learn how to look within and increase their knowledge about volatile issues and how to effectively handle them. They can be catalysts towards deeper integrity, inclusivity, compassion, and understanding.

A word of caution: while we may be tempted to label someone as having a disorder because of our discomfort with them, we need to leave diagnoses and treatments to the professionals. Please keep in mind that being compassionate while keeping your heart and mind open is key to building healthier and more conscious relationships.

Always take care to distinguish compassion from emotional entanglement. Although you may care for individuals who are suffering, you should not attempt to heal them or internalize their suffering. In no way do you serve them by taking on their pain. The best thing you can do is to see them as whole and contributing coworkers. We all have our emotional challenges, and we all deserve respect and the opportunity to be our best selves.

Anxieties and Personality Disorders

Let's go through the anxiety and personality disorders to see how we can recognize and respond to them in a healthy and proactive manner. These are the conditions that you are most likely to encounter at the workplace. I will provide you with a brief definition of each one, and I will cite characters in films or television shows who have the condition.

While these examples may be of assistance, it is important to be aware that the media often portray elevated or intensified examples of a condition for the sake of engaging the audience. Not all sociopaths are Hannibal Lecter (portrayed by Anthony Hopkins) in *Silence of the Lambs*, and not all individuals suffering from borderline personality disorder match the extreme behavior of Alex Forrest (Glenn Close) in *Fatal Attraction*. There are varying degrees of disorder. Some may permit high functioning, while others may be extremely debilitating.

The following table lists the fifteen disorders in alphabetical order. Along with each listing, it will give a short description of each condition and movie, television, or theater references that model the condition. It will then provide you with insights on how that condition might be experienced within the three work relationships: with coworkers, subordinates, and superiors. It also suggests ways of dealing with these individuals.

While I have based this segment on a variety of research sources, I have gleaned a great deal of information on personality disorders from the 2000 book *Toxic Workers: How to Deal with Dysfunctional People on the Job* by Alan A. Cavaiola, PhD, and Neil J. Lavender, PhD. As its title suggests, this valuable resource delves into how to deal with toxicity in the workplace. If you want to learn more, I encourage you to purchase this wonderful book.

Anxiety and Personality Disorders
Interacting with the Three Types of Work Relationships

Antisocial

Persistent antisocial, irresponsible, or criminal behavior, often impulsive or aggressive, without regard for any harm or distress caused to others. Rarely displays remorse and has an inability to maintain long-term social and personal relationships. Cannot always be trusted and are the most at risk for contributing to workplace violence. Movie examples include the Joker in *The Dark Night*, Mr. Spock in the original *Star Trek* series, Alex DeLarge in *A Clockwork Orange*, Tommy DeVito in *Goodfellas*, Hannibal Lecter in *Silence of the Lambs*, and Nicky Santoro in *Casino*.

Antisocial Coworker

CHARACTERISTICS
- Makes coworkers feel responsible for them.
- Takes advantage, especially of the codependent.
- Can be cunningly two-faced in presenting a façade to management.
- Can be ruthlessly manipulative; incapable of emotional intimacy.
- Can con you into doing their work.
- Rejects authority and discipline.

STRATEGIES
- Set strong and healthy boundaries; protect your property.
- Avoid explosive situations and don't take them personally.
- Document issues; ask for help.

Antisocial Subordinate

CHARACTERISTICS
- Can lay claim to others' work without any sense of guilt.
- Can be extremely manipulative and persuasive about their innocence even when guilty.
- Can entangle you in a web of dishonesty and manipulation.
- May appear good at their work, but may show inconsistencies.
- Can cunningly create divisions among staff.

STRATEGIES
- Trust your intuition and gut responses to these individuals.
- Keep someone else in the workplace informed, and check in with them to maintain clarity and objectivity.
- Keep thorough documentation of all interactions.

Antisocial Superior

CHARACTERISTICS
- Dangerously charismatic.
- Can brainwash employees into believing that that they are the problem.
- Subordinates can lose self-esteem as a result of emotional manipulation.
- Can erode subordinates' self-confidence with emotionally abusive tricks.

STRATEGIES
- Avoid power struggles, and set limits from which you do not sway.
- Beware of their social skills and apparent warmth in gestures.
- When possible, provide written communication and allow them time to articulate their response.
- Keep updated work logs and records of communications.
- Build your own inner strength and your sense of self-worth to avoid being triggered.

Avoidant

Anxiety in social situations and personal relationships, with feelings of inadequacy and extreme sensitivity to rejection or criticism. Movie examples: Alex DeLarge (Malcolm McDowell) in *A Clockwork Orange*, William Forester (Sean Connery) in *Finding Forester*, Laura Wingfield (Jane Wyman) in *The Glass Menagerie*.

Avoidant Coworker

CHARACTERISTICS
- Often self-conscious.
- Shies away from activities that require interaction with others.
- May be invisible to you, or may heavily lean on you for support if you have befriended them.
- May try to get you to do their difficult work that deals with confronting others.

STRATEGIES
- Encourage them about their own abilities.
- Support healthy interaction among coworkers.
- Allow them the space to stand up for themselves and avoid doing so for them.

Avoidant Subordinate

CHARACTERISTICS
- Fearful of being negatively evaluated.
- Sees criticism as a personal affront reflecting on their intrinsic value as a person.
- Quiet, unassuming; can be disturbed if introduced to change.

STRATEGIES
- Encourage them with the knowledge that you value them and what they offer.
- Provide them with tasks that gradually expose them to greater challenges.

Avoidant Superior

CHARACTERISTICS

- Rarely in a management position, because they avoid interaction.
- Has difficulty leading and guiding others; noncommittal.
- Tit-for-tat attitude: if you hurt them, they will hurt you back.

STRATEGIES

- Request clarity on expectations and specific deadlines.
- Encourage them in their role. This can help them to better manage you.
- Refrain from revengeful interplay and competitive positioning.

Bipolar

Formerly known as *manic-depressive*. Alternating periods of elation and depression. Difficulty in the workplace due to changing and unpredictable mood swings. Movie and television examples: Pat (Bradley Cooper) in *Silver Lining Playbook*, Carrie Mathison (Claire Danes) in *Homeland*, Ian Gallagher (Cameron Monaghan) in *Shameless*.

SEVEN SIGNS OF MANIA

Mania can cause other symptoms as well, but seven of the key signs of this phase of bipolar disorder are:

1. Feeling overly happy or high for long periods of time
2. A decreased need for sleep
3. Talking very fast, often with racing thoughts
4. Feeling extremely restless or impulsive
5. Becoming easily distracted
6. Overconfidence in one's abilities
7. Engaging in risky behavior, such as having impulsive sex, gambling with life savings, or going on big spending sprees

SEVEN SIGNS OF DEPRESSION

Like mania, depression can cause other symptoms as well, but here are seven of the key signs as manifested in bipolar disorder:

1. Feeling sad or hopeless for long periods of time
2. Withdrawing from friends and family
3. Losing interest in activities that you once enjoyed
4. Having a significant change in appetite
5. Severe fatigue or lack of energy
6. Problems with memory, concentration, and decision making
7. Thinking about or attempting suicide, or having a preoccupation with death

Bipolar Coworker

CHARACTERISTICS
- Can be extremely unpredictable in their behavior.
- Can pull you into caring for them, hindering your work.

STRATEGIES
- Avoid losing yourself in caring for them.
- Avoid becoming engaged in roller coaster of emotions.
- Be compassionate, but separate yourself from their disabilities.

Bipolar Subordinate

CHARACTERISTICS
- Can be affected by the stigma attached to bipolarism.
- Can be inconsistent in performance due to side effects of mood swings.
- Performance can be affected by lethargy or inability to concentrate.
- Can be overconfident of abilities.

STRATEGIES
- Be sure to tackle the stigma.
- Encourage results, but be willing to be flexible with hours and other details.
- Ensure that you have policies and procedures that provide the best possible work environment for all, encouraging life-work balance.
- Offer training or coaching in time management and mental health support.

Bipolar Superior

CHARACTERISTICS
- Can be explosive.
- Can be inconsistent in their management style because of mood swings.
- Can be extreme and inconsistent in responses depending upon mood.

STRATEGIES

- If you are targeted, don't take it personally.
- Focus on the content of what they are saying rather than on their tone.
- Seek out the underlying causes of outbursts so you can remedy them before they escalate.
- Be strategic in creating positive support and building team sensibility.
- Note if you feel overtly bullied, and report their behavior if they have gone too far.

Borderline

Severe mood swings, impulsive behavior, and difficulty in forming stable personal relationships, often related to an intense fear of abandonment or instability. Can result in inappropriate anger, impulsiveness, and frequent mood swings. Can also be egocentric. Movie examples: Alex Forrest (Glenn Close) in *Fatal Attraction* and Susanna Kaysen (Winona Ryder) in *Girl Interrupted.*

Borderline Coworker

CHARACTERISTICS
- Can get under your skin; unstable in personal relationships.
- Can have explosive tempers.
- May go from idolization to hatred of others, from putting others on a pedestal to contempt.
- Irrational fear of abandonment.
- Unclear about who they are or what they want in their lives.
- Exhibits excessive behaviors such as overspending or sexual hyperactivity.

STRATEGIES
- Avoid being pulled into their dramas.
- Avoid rescuing; reflect on your intentions in wanting to do so.
- Avoid engaging in gossip with or about them.

Borderline Subordinate

CHARACTERISTICS
- Unable to work cooperatively with others.
- Ultrasensitive to criticism; paranoid and overreactive.
- Tends to be moody and angry.

STRATEGIES
- Maintain concise and updated records.
- Support projects that require working independently.
- Avoid explosive episodes through calm and concise communication.

Borderline Superior

CHARACTERISTICS

- Often lures staff into becoming too emotionally involved with them.
- Can idolize you, then turn against you.
- Destructive to your physical and emotional health.
- Displays extreme mood swings and creates drama.
- Personalizes situations, making work environment tense.

STRATEGIES

- Don't take the bait.
- Keep a distance, and stay out of personal involvements.
- Keep concise records and base exchanges on facts over emotions.

Dependent

Excessive emotional and practical reliance on other people; inability to make decisions without support; passive or submissive behavior. Movie and television examples: Anney (Jennifer Jason Leigh) in *Bastard out of Carolina*, Bekir (Vildan Atasever) in *Destiny*, Little Edie (Drew Barrymore) in *Grey Gardens*.

People who suffer from dependent personality disorder can be highly loyal and supportive friends, but they can also have a strong reliance upon others. According to the fifth edition of *Diagnostic and Statistical Manual of Mental Disorders*, dependent personality disorder displays eight features:

1. Has difficulty making everyday decisions without an excessive amount of advice and reassurance from others.
2. Needs others to assume responsibility for most major areas of their life.
3. Has difficulty expressing disagreement with others because of fear of loss of support or approval.
4. Has difficulty initiating projects or doing things on their own. This is due to a lack of self-confidence in their own judgment or abilities rather than a lack of motivation or energy.
5. Goes to excessive lengths to obtain nurturance and support from others, to the point of volunteering to do things that are unpleasant.
6. Feels uncomfortable or helpless when alone because of exaggerated fears of being unable to care for themselves.
7. Urgently seeks another relationship as a source of care and support when a close relationship ends.
8. Is unrealistically preoccupied with fears of being left to take care of themselves.

Dependent Coworker

CHARACTERISTICS

- Can be clingy, accommodating, submissive, and indecisive.
- May be hypercompetent, yet may appear insecure and inept.
- Can be highly supportive and loyal.
- May exhibit a distance-pursuit pattern with closer relationships.

STRATEGIES

- Encourage them by providing positive feedback.
- Do not do difficult tasks on their behalf.
- Model your empowered self, and give them space to express feelings and speak their mind.

Dependent Subordinate

CHARACTERISTICS

- Needs appreciation, acceptance, and security.
- Can be hesitant and reluctant about new or unfamiliar projects.

STRATEGIES

- May need gradual training to enforce their security as they grow into their new tasks and responsibilities.
- Provide positive feedback, and use encouraging rhetoric when sharing criticisms.
- Give them space and encourage independence, but let them know that you are available if needed.

Dependent Superior

CHARACTERISTICS

- Unambitious, so if in a management position, probably achieved that level by working hard to please superiors.
- Seeks to build harmony and cooperation among staff.
- Can take things personally.
- Appreciates team effort; listens to ideas but may be slow to act upon them.
- Highly supportive but non-confrontational.
- Encouraging, but when push comes to shove, may not go to bat on your behalf.

STRATEGIES

- Reassure them of your support.
- Build their trust in you and your abilities.
- Avoid using a confrontational tone when dealing with issues.

Generalized Anxiety

Excessive or unrealistic anxiety about two or more aspects of life (such as work, social relationships, or financial matters). Causes and risk factors include: a family history of anxiety; recent or prolonged exposure to stressful situations, including personal or family illnesses; childhood abuse; or excessive use of caffeine or tobacco (which can worsen existing anxiety). Symptoms can include palpitations, shortness of breath, or dizziness. Can suffer from constant worry, restlessness, and trouble with concentration. Television examples: Randall (Sterling K. Brown) in *This Is Us* and Jean-François Gariépy (playing himself) in *The Twisted Mind of Jean- François Gariépy*.

Anxious Coworker

CHARACTERISTICS
- May find it difficult to concentrate; may pull you away from your work to focus on their issues.
- May display stress-related physical issues; may ask you to help carry their workload.
- Can take additional sick days and be absent, interfering with productivity.

STRATEGIES
- Maintain healthy boundaries; avoid trying to solve their problems.
- Avoid telling them not to worry. This adds to anxiety,
- Be patient.

Anxious Subordinate

CHARACTERISTICS
- Can lack focus and be less productive.
- Can be perfectionistic and extremely self-critical.
- Can have a lot of what-if fears about potential future situations.

STRATEGIES

- Build a wellness plan for them.
- Let them know that you are supportive; create a safe place for them to ask for help.
- Give them space and remain calm when attacks occur.
- Encourage one-on-one conversations instead of gossip and talking about other people.
- Use neutral or positive language and avoid validating negative statements.

Anxious Superior

CHARACTERISTICS

- Can be explosive and reactive if overwhelmed.
- Can push staff beyond healthy limits with workloads.

STRATEGIES

- Focus on what you appreciate about them; let them know you respect them.
- Avoid making assumptions. Ask open-ended questions to better understand their thoughts, needs and concerns.
- Give them space when having difficulty concentrating.
- Find ways that you can support them if they have extreme workload.
- Keep them informed about your work. The more in the know they feel, the less anxiety they will experience.
- Avoid labeling and stigmas.

Histrionic

Excessive attention seeking, emotional overreaction, inappropriately seductive behavior, overdramatization, and excessive need for approval. Movie examples: Regina George (Rachel McAdams) in *Mean Girls* and Mavis Gary (Charlize Theron) in *Young Adult*.

Histrionic Coworker

CHARACTERISTICS
- Can be fun and entertaining, but also energetically draining.
- Can seduce you into engaging in their dramas, or in covering for them as they deal with their dramas.
- Can easily seduce coworker of the opposite sex into covering for them.
- Dramas and storytelling can pull you from your work if you let it.

STRATEGIES
- Avoid confrontations with them; maintain healthy boundaries.
- Make note of your energy and step away when needed.
- Avoid getting pulled into their web of drama and gossip.

Histrionic Subordinate

CHARACTERISTICS
- Can be entertaining, but are rarely organized or focused enough to complete quality work.
- Can drain others with their personal dramas.
- Not always the best workers, because they are often more focused on their internal world over work goals.

STRATEGIES
- Maintain healthy boundaries.
- Be specific about goals and check in on progress on a regular basis.
- Keep conversations professional and do not engage in office drama.
- Provide training on time management and organizational best practices.

Histrionic Superior

CHARACTERISTICS

- Emotionally volatile, overreactive, extreme mood swings.
- Good at selling themselves; may take credit for your efforts.
- May not focus on either your errors or your efforts; may get lost in their own dramas.
- Charismatic.
- Disorganized.
- Unreliable.

STRATEGIES

- Avoid being pulled into their dramas.
- Ask for clear goals and deadlines; check in to ensure organization.
- Keep detailed records of your work accomplishments and completion dates.

Narcissistic

Exaggerated sense of self-importance; need for admiration; lack of empathy for other people. Movie examples: Jasmine (Cate Blanchett) in *Blue Jasmine*, Colonel Nathan Jessup (Jack Nicholson) in *A Few Good Men*, Dennis Reynolds (Glenn Howerton) in *It's Always Sunny in Philadelphia*.

Narcissistic Coworker

CHARACTERISTICS

- Disrespectful and misusing of property.
- Insensitive to others' needs; self-involved.
- Focused on looking good and unwilling to step up; expects you to do so.
- Believes rules don't apply to them.
- Self-directed rather than team- or business-directed.
- Looking good is a priority.

STRATEGIES

- Avoid confrontations or competition.
- Work independently of them when possible.
- If you need to work together, clearly define roles and responsibilities and keep management informed of your efforts and progress.

Narcissistic Subordinate

CHARACTERISTICS

- Disobedient; ignores rules, believing they don't apply to them.
- Can be two-faced (arrogant with you, then repentant with your superior).
- Little to no sense of loyalty.
- Can be hard-working, but with the intent to get to the top in whatever way they can.

STRATEGIES

- When possible, have other management present as witnesses.
- Keep detailed records of conversations and work progress.
- Don't take self-involvement and lack of empathy personally.

Narcissistic Superior

CHARACTERISTICS

- Inaccessible.
- Caustic.
- Need for power.
- Believe rules don't apply to them.
- Driven by their own needs over yours.
- High expectations, with little recognition.
- Can take credit for your good ideas.
- Not thoughtful.
- Uses power inappropriately (such as harassment).

STRATEGIES

- Avoid power struggles. Have witnesses at key meetings.
- Avoid engaging in volatile exchanges.
- Keep others in management team aware of your efforts and progress.

Obsessive-Compulsive Disorder (OCD)

Excessive orderliness, perfectionism, attention to details, and a need for control in relating to others. Examples from movies and television: Hannah (Lena Dunham) in *Girls,* Alex (Dev Patel) in *The Road Within*; Adrian Monk (Tony Shalboub) in *Monk*; Marina (Marina Vasileva) in *Beware of Dog*; Bob Wiley (Bill Murray) in *What about Bob*; Howard Hughes (Leonardo DiCaprio) in *The Aviator.*

Obsessive-Compulsive Coworker

CHARACTERISTICS
- Can be excellent in a position like quality control.
- Compulsivity may try the patience of others.
- May require additional time to complete tasks.

STRATEGIES
- Maintain positive communication; encourage and support.
- Emphasize teamwork; be optimistic and set clear goals.
- Try not to take criticisms personally.
- Hold to your own objectives; be careful not to be swayed by theirs.

Obsessive-Compulsive Subordinate

CHARACTERISTICS
- Can be extremely committed.
- Can be excellent in a position like quality control.

STRATEGIES
- Be careful they don't get lost or behind because of details; keep them moving forward.
- Be specific, encouraging, and direct when providing guidance.
- Allow flexible hours and frequent short breaks.
- Keep lines of communication open, positive, and supportive.
- Can be overfunctioning, so be sure to set realistic goals and ensure they adhere to them.

Obsessive-Compulsive Superior

CHARACTERISTICS

- Can be tough and not always emotionally supportive.
- Can be extremely controlling; tend to micromanage because of their anxiety.
- Can be highly efficient, with excellent work ethic.

STRATEGIES

- Set healthy boundaries; set aside private time, and make your limits clear.
- Seek support from human resources department if you are being overscheduled, overcriticized, or passed over for opportunities.
- Be clear and succinct in communication; avoid seeking praise.

Panic Disorder

Recurring unexpected panic attacks—sudden periods of intense fear that may include palpitations, sweating, shaking, shortness of breath, numbness, or a feeling that something terrible is going to happen. Movie examples: Jasmine (Cate Blanchette) in *Blue Jasmine*; Patrick (Lucas Hedges) in *Manchester by the Sea*; Kayla (Elsie Fisher) in *Eighth Grade*.

Coworker with Panic Disorder

CHARACTERISTICS
- Can experience panic when stressed or triggered.
- Can be loyal, committed, and hard-working.

STRATEGIES
- May need reassurance and security to perform their best.
- Inform them that you support them and that they are safe.
- Remain calm when they have attack; give them their space.

Subordinate with Panic Disorder

CHARACTERISTICS
- Can be nervous and easily overwhelmed.
- Needs to feel understood and supported by you.
- Can panic under stress.
- Can be very loyal, especially when feeling appreciated, safe, and understood.

STRATEGIES
- Treat them with sensitivity, encouragement, and a gentle hand.
- Avoid exposing them to long work hours, excessive workloads, unreasonable targets, or prolonged pressure.
- Keep other staff knowledgeable about panic attacks and how to best support coworkers when attacks arise.
- Create wellness action plans to support awareness of their needs.

Superior with Panic Disorder

CHARACTERISTICS

- Can be volatile, stressed, and easily triggered.
- May need to be encouraged that you are loyal and have their back.
- Can be highly functional when feeling secure and supported.
- Generally sensitive to workers' needs, but can be preoccupied with their own uneasiness.

STRATEGIES

- Engage in constructive and supportive conversations; offer to bring herbal tea, water, or another soothing, noncaffeinated drink.
- Stay calm and resist responding when they are agitated.
- Ask if you can take messages or respond to emails to support them when they need uninterrupted time.

Paranoid

Exaggerated distrust and suspicion of other people. Movie examples: John Nash (Russell Crowe) in *A Beautiful Mind*; various characters in *Paranoid*.

Paranoid Coworker

CHARACTERISTICS

- Can be highly competitive and suspicious of your intentions and actions.

STRATEGIES

- Avoid confrontations or debates: they can lead to stress and additional paranoid behavior.
- Be careful about criticizing them; encourage and cooperate.

Paranoid Subordinate

CHARACTERISTICS

- Can be difficult to manage, especially when discussing the quality of their work.
- Tends to be risk-averse.

STRATEGIES

- Be clear, concise, and positive in your feedback.
- When critiquing, be gentle. Emphasize their positive traits and underplay the negative ones.
- You may need to treat them with kid gloves; misunderstandings can be exaggerated and misinterpreted.

Paranoid Superior

CHARACTERISTICS

- Hypervigilant about staff loyalty; very aware and suspicious of competing businesses.
- Distrusting of staff; needs to feel in control.
- Can micromanage, distrusting others to adequately perform tasks.

STRATEGIES

- Avoid challenging or questioning them.
- Avoid taking risks or trying new things without their prior approval.
- Keep them well informed about your progress.
- Do not take micromanaging or defensive behaviors personally.

Passive-Aggressive

Indirectly expressing negative feelings, instead of openly addressing them. Shift blame and can avoid picking up their share of the workload. Movie examples: Emma Allan (Anne Hathaway) and Liv Lerner (Kate Hudson) in *Bride Wars*, Jane Nichols (Katherine Heigl) in *27 Dresses*, Brooke Meyers (Jennifer Aniston) and Gary Grobowski (Vince Vaughn) in *The Break-up*, the Captain (James Cagney) in *Mister Roberts*, Mrs. Laura Cheveley (Julianne Moore) in *An Ideal Husband*, and Jack Byrnes (Robert de Niro) in *Meet the Parents*.

Passive-Aggressive Coworker

CHARACTERISTICS

- Complains about being victimized and treated unfairly by others.
- Tends to procrastinate and miss deadlines.
- Takes the path of least resistance in regard to effort, commitment to doing quality work, and promptness.
- If partnered with you, can ignore your communications and efforts and in the end lay claim to your efforts.

STRATEGIES

- Try to understand motivation (often fear).
- Avoid overreacting or lashing out.
- Be honest; practice radical candor (being honest while kind).
- Avoid future issues by building a relationship in which they trust.

Passive-Aggressive Subordinate

CHARACTERISTICS

- Can be tardy, late in completing work, and full of excuses when they do not pull their weight.
- Tends to point their finger at you or coworkers when things go wrong or when they are criticized.

STRATEGIES

- May need incentives and bargaining to meet deadlines: "If you complete X by Y, I will give you Z."
- Angry responses only fuel passive-aggressive behaviors. Stay calm, and keep concise documents to support your efforts and their lack thereof.
- Calmly discuss the core issue and avoid giving credence to the toxicity.

Passive-Aggressive Superior

CHARACTERISTICS

- Rarely aspires to managerial positions. They are not driven to succeed—in fact, quite the opposite.
- Intentionally unreliable. For example, they may lose an important document you created and left on their desk to review.
- Often late for meetings, miss deadlines, or fail to complete paperwork in a timely manner.
- May claim to review your requests and then never do so.
- Often sabotages the efforts of others in subtle but effective ways.

STRATEGIES

- Avoid replicating their passive-aggressive behavior.
- Avoid publicly calling them out. Make the relationship feel safe.
- Keep detailed records of your work efforts and progress.
- Avoid personality issues, and focus on your performance.

Posttraumatic Stress Disorder (PTSD)

A psychiatric disorder that can occur in people who have experienced or witnessed a traumatic event such as a natural disaster, a serious accident, a terrorist act, war or combat, rape, or other violent personal assault. Movie and television examples: Jessica Jones (Krysten Ritter) in *Jessica Jones*, Edgar (Desmin Borges) in *You're the Worst*, Charlie (Logan Lerman) in *The Perks of Being a Wallflower*, Chris Kyle (Bradley Cooper) in *American Sniper*, Ron Kovic (Tom Cruise) in *Fourth of July*.

Coworker with PTSD

CHARACTERISTICS

- Can be triggered by stress or other situations that cause anxiety.
- Can behave inconsistently—at times highly reliable and committed, at other times unable to function because of anxieties.
- Can be empathetic and sensitive to colleagues' needs.

STRATEGIES

- Indicate potentially jarring actions beforehand (for example, tell them when you are going to open the door and avoid tapping them on the shoulder from behind).
- Give them space and allow them to make decisions at their pace.
- Avoid trivializing; this *is* a valid medical condition.

Subordinate with PTSD

CHARACTERISTICS

- May need to be treated with gentle sensitivity; needs to feel secure and supported.
- Can require space and emotional support for relief when triggered.
- Can be very loyal, especially when you are sensitive to their needs.
- May need reassurance that they are doing good work and that they are not judged for their PTSD.

STRATEGIES

- Train all staff about warning signs.
- Create work duty checklists, memory aids, or timers.
- Create workplace wellness program encouraging exercise and stress reduction techniques and practices.
- Allow for flexible schedule and scheduled rest breaks.

Superior with PTSD

CHARACTERISTICS

- Can be highly functional when not triggered.
- Can have outbursts of panic when faced with extreme stress.
- Can be highly sensitive and supportive to workers' needs.
- Can struggle with feelings of being out of control.

STRATEGIES

- Support them in feeling safe and supported; will be very supportive in turn.
- Keep them informed and abreast of your progress.
- Be cognizant of triggers and avoid creating unnecessary stress.
- Allow idiosyncrasies and show compassion, respect, and support.

Schizoid

Lack of interest in social or intimate relationships; difficulty with expressing emotions; prefer a solitary or sheltered lifestyle. Movie examples: John Nash (Russell Crowe) in *A Beautiful Mind*, Travis Black (Robert DeNiro) in *Taxi*, Gollum (Andy Serkis) in *The Lord of the Rings* and *The Hobbit*.

Schizoid Coworker

CHARACTERISTICS

- May have little self-awareness.
- May have difficulty communicating.
- Can be socially inept; unable to understand rules of social etiquette and emotionally disconnected; distant.
- Solitary; does not enjoy relationships; shows little interest in pleasure.
- Can be emotionally cold and detached; indifferent to praise or criticism.

STRATEGIES

- Give them space; do not feel socially obligated to include them.
- Use technology as an unobtrusive way to connect.

Schizoid Subordinate

CHARACTERISTICS

- Has difficulty describing others; uses short, nondescript responses.
- Self-sufficient; often has technical rather than relational prowess.
- Can be very independent but not highly ambitious.

STRATEGIES

- Ask open-ended questions as opposed to "yes" or "no."
- Can prefer to work alone; if so, do not force social interactions.

Schizoid Superior

CHARACTERISTICS

- Provides staff with little or no direction.
- Insensitive to staff's emotional or personal needs.
- Can display angry outbursts or indirect aggression toward staff.
- Often remedies issues in punitive ways, unaware of effect on employees.

STRATEGIES

- Emphasize logic rather than using emotional words in communicating.
- It may be helpful to share ideas among subordinates to solve problems and air grievances.

Social Phobia

Intense anxiety or fear of being judged, negatively evaluated, or rejected in a social or performance situation. Examples from movies and the stage: Evan Hansen (Ben Platt) in *Dear Evan Hansen*, Natalie (Lori Smith) in *Meltdown*.

Coworker with Social Phobia

CHARACTERISTICS
- Can be highly sensitive and suspicious of how others might judge them.
- Can be withdrawn and awkward in social situations.
- Most likely prefers to work alone and avoids interacting with others.
- Can become fearful of being undermined.

STRATEGIES
- Be a collaborative champion. Use encouragement and support.
- Avoid enabling, and gently support them in facing fears.

Subordinate with Social Phobia

CHARACTERISTICS
- Can be defensive when given feedback on work performance.
- Withdraws from social activity; does not like working in a team.
- Tends to be passive and works independently.

STRATEGIES
- Set realistic goals and support them in overcoming obstacles.
- Be clear in communication, provide questions in advance of meetings.
- Support them in managing perfectionism; provide ongoing encouragement.

Superior with Social Phobia

CHARACTERISTICS
- Tends to provide staff with very little direction.
- Can be highly indecisive for fear of being wrong.
- Can avoid being direct and specific in instructions for fear of being judged.
- May create tension for staff for fear of being judged as inadequate by superiors.

STRATEGIES
- Provide concise and clear communications of your intentions and efforts.
- Be direct in communication and avoid gossip and triangles.
- Be honest and up-front, especially around expectations and deadlines.

Tips for Responding to Others with Anxiety or PDs

Here are signs of ego responses to anxiety or personality disorders, along with some tips that can support greater functionality and more intimate connections with colleagues are challenged with them.

THE EGO'S RESPONSE

- You immediately label them and judge them as less than you because of their disorder. Labels are limiting and can be fear-based ways of trying to compartmentalize what we don't fully understand. We are much more than our illnesses, and life can be much more complex than we realize. Often we label as a means of maintaining control when we feel powerless. Know this, and try to be present rather than disconnected and diagnostic.

- You mock them and gossip about them as a means of pseudoconnection with fellow coworkers. While some of the dramas may be amusing, connecting with others at the expense of someone who is suffering is negative in every way. It erodes both the sense of community and connection in the business and your own self-respect.

- You use their disability for your own gains. For example, you might undermine their efforts and encourage your manager to give you a high-profile project because you are "better qualified." Such deceptive behavior will eventually catch up with you.

- You may triangle (get a third party involved in your disputes). This is tempting when you are building a case (especially when you are feeling doubtful about yourself), but pulling others into the situation creates more of a mess to clean up later. Please note, however, that if you are being emotionally abused, it is important that you take care of your needs and inform management or human resources of the situation.

- You may project your own issues and prejudices on them. You might do this by perceiving them as weak or lacking courage because they have the illness, or suggesting that they could cure it if only they had the willpower and stamina to do so.

- You may rush to heal others, becoming their sounding board and advice giver. You tell yourself that we are kind and thoughtful, that you just want to be there for them. In fact, very often you become a caregiver for others as a means of avoiding your own fears and anxieties.

- You may alienate them, increasing their sense of uneasiness at the workplace. In this case you are the problem in the workplace, not them!

THE HEART'S RESPONSE

- See the individual in light of the complete soul that they are. Viewing them as wounded does not serve either you or them. It keeps them limited and doesn't allow them the space to grow.

- Hold them accountable to the rules and regulations outlined for all staff, respecting them as capable, functioning contributors. At the same time, be flexible and willing to support them in ways that honor their challenges, while motivating, encouraging, and uplifting them.

- Cultivate compassion and acceptance. The more you can feel loving kindness towards them, the more they feel it, and the more you will experience deeper love and respect towards yourself.

- Maintain healthy boundaries. While remaining compassionate and kind, do not take on their energy (or anyone else's for that matter). If you are an empath, you often absorb the energy of those around you without realizing it. At the end of the day you are exhausted. Your exhaustion can come from taking on the troubles of those around you. Set a strong intention to be compassionate and kind without losing energy.

• Avoid trying to give advice. Know that seeing the other as able to deal with their problems gives them the space to do just that. When you try to "fix" others, you disempower them.

• When you note that they are being triggered (or if you find yourself being triggered), do the "yes" process. See your heart filling with loving, white light and expanding outward to fill your entire body. Then see it expanding to fill their hearts and the hearts of all others in the office. You don't have to wait until triggers occur. Doing this practice every day will set the tone for higher consciousness to permeate your work environment.

THE WITNESS-SELF'S RESPONSE

In his YouTube video *What Is the Purpose of Mental Illness?* Eckhart Tolle states that we think we are autonomous, but we are not. We are one consciousness, and the flowering of our consciousness as humankind evolves through the obstacles. He says:

> What we see as somebody's personal identity is not who they are. They are an expression of the One, which is constantly finding new channels

through which to express itself in this world. So, if this channel is blocked, we see it as a person who is suffering—that's also true on one level. Of course, you help in whatever way you can. That personal sense of self is ultimately an illusion because who you are is ultimately timeless, beyond the illusion. If I had not encountered all these seeming blockages in my life, I would not be here now. . . . the obstacles to the arising of consciousness are ultimately part of the arising consciousness, and there is only one life. . . . You are an expression of the One and everybody is. . . . All of the blockages and all the suffering actually were part of the awakening without which it would not have happened. Collectively the suffering of humanity is also a necessary part of the awakening.

From an enlightened perspective, we are not individuals but a part of the whole, the One. From blockages comes the flowering of our consciousness. Although it is difficult and painful, it is from this place that our consciousness is raised.

While I can only speak for myself, I know that my path towards self-discovery started with road rage. When I noted deep anger and pain, I sought help. Had I not experienced the pain, I never would have sought solace, resolve, or deeper understanding. After several years of therapy, I noted that by cutting off the pain in my life, I was also cutting off the joy. When I found safe ways to explore my issues and feel into the pain, I also discovered the joy that I had shut down when I repressed the pain.

When a Person Does Not See Their Illness

It can be difficult to be in the presence of someone who is unaware of their mental illness or of the part they play in creating a toxic work environment. Having been in such situations, I can assure you that attempting to convince them of their role in the unhealthy environment is futile. I have journeyed down that road, and it only led to frustration, criticism, and anxiety within me. I wasted my time and energy, and I may have even pulled the person further away from self-disclosure through my sheer will to force them into owning their part. I am sure you have heard the saying, "What you think about me is none of my business." In this case, what you think about them is none of your business. In other words, it is not your place to convince another of their strengths or weaknesses, health or maladies.

There is a saying in *A Course in Miracles* that is one of the most powerful I have ever heard: "There are only two choices in life—fear or love." As you try to convince another of the part they play in any wrongdoing, you might ask yourself, "Do I want to be right (in fear), or do I want to choose love?" If you choose love, you will focus on your own personal growth, and love the other where they are. This doesn't mean that you should allow them to bully, manipulate, or abuse you in any way. But it does mean that you are not put on this earth to be the judge and jury of others. The more you judge others, the more you become aware of your own inner judge. The more you criticize outside of yourself, the more you are unwilling to look within.

When You May Not See
Your Own Mental Illness

During a meditation, I saw Jesus standing in front of a mentally ill individual, saying, "I see you, and I love you." As I watched, the armor of the man's mental illness began to fall from his weighted body. Once fully removed, he became an open-hearted and healthy little boy.

We all want to be seen and understood, but what if we can't see ourselves? What if our walls of protection are so thick that we ourselves cannot infiltrate them?

Sometimes it is difficult to see the part that we play in a toxic environment, especially when we are in the midst of the drama. We may need months or even years of separation from the situation before clarity sets in. Setting a strong intention for clarity with the commitment to be fully honest with ourselves about the part we played (or didn't play) in the drama invites courage, clarity, and release. Insights, observations, and awareness will bubble out of our unconscious and into our conscious thoughts and feelings in order to be rectified and healed.

When I reflect back on the time when I was going through a difficult personal situation, I can see how much my toxic thoughts and my sense of being overwhelmed were affecting my coworkers. Although I did my job and delivered quality work to the company, I can recall a number of times when I was in the boss's office, sharing my stories of woe, or lunching with a friend, crying in my soup over my personal drama. At that time, I was blind to the toxicity of my emotional outbursts. In retrospect, I can now see that they had no place in the office. My rants were inappropriate and did not reflect the light of who I really am. They were unprofessional and a distraction. In fact, they were a hindrance to the relationship I had built with my immediate manager.

If you are unsure whether you are struggling with mental illness, anxiety, personality disorders, or depression, I encourage you to take the time to investigate. Go to a therapist or social worker, take some assessment tests, and be willing to face yourself. As I previously mentioned, my desire to understand the road rage I was feeling has taken me on a journey of self-discovery and self-acceptance that has been a deep blessing in my life. Sticking your head in the sand and maintaining a stance of angry victim will bring nothing but further heartache and pain. The more you have the courage to face yourself in all of your perfect imperfection, the more you will fall in love with yourself. After all, isn't our life's journey about falling deeply in love with ourselves and those around us? When we open to the love that comes from deep introspection, deeper compassion, and even deeper forgiveness, we open to experiencing complete and utter joy in our lives. What more could we ask for?

Harnessing the Power of Forgiveness

As we commit to fully owning our part in any toxic situation, it is important to forgive ourselves and the others involved. I have finally come to the place where I have forgiven myself for my rants. I recently apologized to my dear colleague, Susan, whom I constantly barraged with my "He said . . . she said . . . I said . . ." rants. Although she told me that forgiveness was not necessary and that she was happy to be there to support me, I know that an apology was necessary. I did the best that I could at that time (if I knew better, I would have done better), but I still believe that my rants took an energetic toll on Susan. In the end, I loved myself more for owning my rants and sharing my apology. Doing so elevated me to a state of massive gratitude for Susan and her steadfast friendship. Gratitude is powerful and transformative. Had I not apologized to her, I would not have been led to the huge, joyful place of gratitude for our friendship. Ultimately, the act of apologizing elevated the energy to the place where miracles are planted.

Beware of False Forgiveness

Forgiveness is a wonderful—even self-full—practice that helps us release toxicity and move forward. But it does not mean that someone else's hurtful actions were OK. We may never forgive the behavior; we may also be unable to truly forgive anyone at the time of the situation.

We should never impose forgiveness when it is inauthentic and coming from a place of "I should . . ." That is false forgiveness. In this case, you would not be truly forgiving, because this impulse is shame-based at its core. If your will to forgive is not heartfelt but comes from the place of "I need to do this because it's bad not to forgive" or "I am told by friends, family, religion, culture (or any other external force) that I need to forgive," the forgiveness will not be true, authentic, or heart-based. It will be an externally driven, fear-based, egoic act. When we follow this impetus, we are afraid of being unloving if we do not forgive. Therefore our need to forgive is based in our fear of being unlovable, of being shamed in this world or the next. True forgiveness has to be authentic and has to come in its own time.

At the same time, setting an intention to forgive at some point thereafter gets the ball rolling and starts to clear your path towards it. You will know when you are ready to forgive. Set a strong intention to release the pain around the situation. Allow your heart to lead, and have faith that when it is time, your heart will provide you with the insights, signals, and means by which you can start on your forgiveness journey.

Finding My Way Out of an Asocial Quagmire

Sometimes you are unable to work issues out with an individual, no matter how hard you try or how much you are committed to doing so. Even so, remaining

firm with your intention to find a resolution is important, and staying open to signs, signals, and guidance
can be key. When you do, sometimes remedies can
appear in the oddest of ways.

Case in point: when I was a producer at Nightingale-
Conant, I went through a situation with someone who
was behaving in an asocial manner (I don't believe
his behavior was as extreme as antisocial). We were
recording an audiobook with a reputable author, and
on several occasions the engineer argued with me in
response to requests that I was making as the producer. I was shocked and found it embarrassing (as
he questioned my choices in front of the author). After
the recording session was over, I approached him and
asked, "Is there something I did that annoyed you in
the session? Is there a protocol or practice that I was
not correctly following?" His response was, "No. You
did nothing. I just don't like people." I left the conversation thinking, "Now what? How do I work with
that?"

Within the month I was to record a program with
a top inspirational speaker. It was going to be the first
one-on-one, in-studio interaction for this author; previously she would only allow us to record live events.
So this was a big deal. I was assigned to be her producer, and I wanted to make the recording experience
outstanding for all. However, given the response of
the engineer (who was also scheduled to record this
session), I didn't know how to prevent toxic interactions during the two days of recording.

I did something that was highly unconventional. While I can't guarantee that it will work for you, it certainly worked for me. I left the day of our discussion thinking, "Well, I can't work with his personality-self. I tried and got a response that I could not work with. What if I work with his soul-self?" So each evening before going to sleep, I would have a conversation with his soul-self. It went something like this, "Hey, engineer's soul. I have a situation here, and I really need your help! I've got a recording session coming up in three weeks, and I'm really nervous about it. I really want it to work out. I humbly ask you to work with his personality-self so that we can connect soul to soul and ease the tension. I want the recording to go really smoothly. I want the energy to be warm, welcoming, and joyful. I humbly and gratefully ask for your help."

I'd never attempted anything like this before, but I was guided from within to do so. And guess what? It worked. The morning of the recording he was peaches-and-cream friendly. The session went without a hitch, and I was awestruck and filled with gratitude. So I suggest that the next time you are confronted with someone who is closed to conscious and open conversation, you might work with their soul-self.

Change Your Mind, Not Theirs
Ultimately each circumstance is unique, and each individual you will come in contact with will respond differently. There is no blanket response that guaran-

tees success with others. Some many have more than one mental health issue, and others may have slight disorders that barely affect their work efforts. To end this chapter, I want to share a story with you that I found both fascinating and inspiring.

I was privileged to be able to work from home when I was employed at Nightingale-Conant Corporation. I had a new baby, and traveling to and from the office was lengthy. With the exception of audio recording sessions and weekly production meetings, I could do all of my writing, editing, and producing work on my laptop. After several years of working from home, the vice president of the company called me into his office.

After some idle chitchat, he informed me that I could no longer work from home. I was very disappointed and asked why. "Did something happen? Are you unhappy with the quality of my work?" He responded, "No, Theresa. Not at all. In fact, you are one of our hardest-working employees. It's not that. It's just that several employees also asked to work from home, and frankly, many don't have the discipline to do so. You've started a precedent that we cannot follow with all employees."

My first response was to close my heart and get angry. While I respected the vice president and completely understood why he made this decision, I immediately went into defensive mode (ego-based thinking). I started to build a case for making him the enemy (while I knew logically he was not). I immediately realized that taking an adversarial stance to his decision would serve no one, especially me. So I asked if he would give me a week, after which time we could reconvene. He agreed.

During that week, I observed my ego. It was cunning, defensive, and contriving. I knew that it was up to no good, and I knew that I had to change my perspective on the situation. I was bound and determined to quell the angry "I am a victim and he is the enemy" case that I was building for myself. So each day I would focus on everything that I respected about him. For the entire week, I worked on changing my mind about him.

Finally, the day of our second meeting arrived. I left my home feeling very different than I did a week ago. I felt a greater sense of respect and appreciation for the vice president. I was resolved to work from home, and I really didn't have an agenda. No sooner had I walked into his office that he exclaimed, "Theresa, what have you done? You're different somehow. I've never seen you so calm!" There was a short pause, and before I could respond he said, "You know what? We don't need to have this discussion. Just keep working from home. I'll deal with your coworkers as needed." End of story.

Please note that all I did was change my mind about him. I consciously decided not to make him the enemy and not to turn the situation into an angry, adversarial one. In response to changing my mind, the energy of the situation was transformed. So next time you are tempted to have an ego-based dialogue, I encourage you to step away, take a break, breathe, feel into your feelings around the issue as they arise, and see where they lead you. In this case, they led me to choose a different, more proactive response. After all, in the end we cannot change others. All we can do is change ourselves. When even one individual makes a shift, the relationship will change. It has to. That's the law of cause and effect.

When It Might Be Time to Leave

At some point, you may question whether staying at your current position will further support you and your work. You may feel that you have given your all, but that you are no longer a fit with the organization. You may have outgrown them, they may have outgrown you, or you may not have been a good match from the start. If you are in a toxic work environment, staying may inevitably pull you into the toxicity.

Here are some guideposts and exercises that may assist you in deciding whether you should stay or go. Some potential signs that you are done:

You discover that you have lost yourself in the environment you are in. In certain situations, I found myself so angry and feeling so victimized that I hated the person I had become. I worked on these feelings. I spoke to therapists and did as much personal work as I could. Nevertheless, I was still angry and feeling victimized. In truth, we are never victims, but I had difficulty pulling myself from that frame of mind.

When this is the case, do an emotional inventory and ask yourself:

- "What was my role in the drama, and what was theirs? What am I accountable for?" Write a list, and journal about the situation in order to gain deeper clarity.

- "Why was I so triggered? Is there a part of me that I need to honestly look at so that I don't recreate this scenario again in my life?"

- "What can I do to heal the wounds that I have around this situation?"

After doing a great deal of emotional inventory work, you may decide to leave. Continue to look within and to work on the triggers that had been activated at that job. If you don't, they will likely reappear again.

Another warning sign is an erosion of your self-esteem. This is tricky, because you may have been so emotionally abused that you believe that you are the problem and that you have nothing to offer a business.

Check in with your heart, and ask for clarity. Breathe into opening your heart, and ask, "Has my sense of self been eroded here? Please help me find clarity about the part I played. Help me to see that which I may be making myself responsible for, although I am not." Then listen carefully and heed the heart-directed guidance.

Another sign is that you dread going into work each day. If so, ask yourself why you feel such dread. Is the environment around you toxic, or is the toxicity within you? If you discover that the toxicity is mostly prevalent in the work environment, perhaps it is time to go.

Another indication that it might be time to leave is that you bring your anger, resentment, and feelings of powerlessness home and lash out at your family and friends. If you are struggling with family members because of angry outbursts and impatience stemming from your job, again, perhaps it is time to leave.

Still another sign is that you are unable to sleep at night because you are worrying about your job and the day ahead. If you are ruminating for hours each night, so worked up that you are unable to sleep, it might be time to find a position that is better suited for you.

Another symptom is that you find yourself incessantly sharing crazy-making work stories with your friends and family. Your life is so consumed with the chaos, confusion, and injustice of the situation that you are unable to let go of it during your personal time. If you tend to worry and ruminate over work situations wherever you are, then perhaps the challenge is not external but lies within. If this is the case, continue to investigate your worrisome ways and look at your fears squarely. Feel into those fears as opposed to repressing them. Experiencing them fully will lead you in the direction you need to go in.

Energetic depletion is another sign. You may only be a couple of hours into your workday but find it difficult to stay awake. While this could be a sign of a physical ailment, it could also indicate that your workplace is draining you energetically. You may want to get a physical assessment. If the exhaustion is emotional from being in a toxic environment, you may wish to move on.

Also observe whether the quality of your work is diminishing because you are energetically drained. If you are usually very focused, but feel unfocused and unable to complete your tasks in this work environment, perhaps it's time to forge a new path elsewhere.

Note also if your coworkers are energetic vampires. Check in after having conversations with them. Do you feel energized or emotionally drained afterward? If the bulk of your work relationships leave you feeling drained, then perhaps it is time to find a team that is more affirming and supports your efforts to raise your inner consciousness.

Observe also whether you are confused, troubled, and unsure of what your next step should be. Ask your highest self for guidance: "Is there something I need to see? Is there a lesson that I need to learn?" After doing this emotional inventory, ask that any confusion be cleared. Ask for the insights that can propel you into the next step that you need to take.

Pay attention if you get a gut feeling that tells you, "It's time to leave." Don't fight a losing battle because of your sense of loyalty. Know that while at the job, you did your best and gave your all, and that is enough. You will win no lifetime achievement medals for going down with a sinking ship. Nothing and no one is worth the price of losing your emotional or mental health. To support you in finding the courage to leave, you might want to write a self-acknowledgment letter, listing the ways in which you contributed to the company's well-being.

After leaving, you may wish to do an energetic cleanse. Envision the heavy, toxic energy leaving your body or any place that might be affected. See it being transmuted into something positive and uplifting, something that enhances the world energetically.

Habit 8

NEUTRALIZE Negativity

*Negativity feeds upon itself. The more negative you are,
the more you will experience negativity in your life. When
you are informed and set an intention for conscious
communication, gossip and negative talk fall away,
and you are left with a new growth, complete
with the burgeoning buds of what could be.*

One in four of your coworkers likely suffers from anxiety disorder or stress-related illness. It can be very difficult to remain neutral and avoid being pulled into the disharmony, but it is integral to your peace of mind. Neutralizing negativity is no easy feat and can take its toll if you don't have enough knowledge and tools to do so. Being aware of your own inner triggers, along with consciously and strategically responding to the mental disorders of others, will ultimately provide you with a great deal more peace of mind.

Conscious Communication Profile

Conscious communication is one of the most powerful ways to shift your consciousness and shift the environment of your workplace. Learning just how conscious your communication style is (or is not) can give you greater clarity about how effective you are and how you might become more so. For each of the questions below, choose the number that most closely aligns with your current communication capabilities (1 being "not at all" and 10 being "a great deal").

1. Do you find it easy to be present and listen attentively to others when they speak to you?
1 — 2 — 3 — 4 — 5 — 6 — 7 — 8 — 9 — 10

2. Are you able to articulate your point of view easily and effortlessly?
1 — 2 — 3 — 4 — 5 — 6 — 7 — 8 — 9 — 10

3. Are you able to listen to others without trying to "fix" them?
1 — 2 — 3 — 4 — 5 — 6 — 7 — 8 — 9 — 10

4. Do you use language that is gentle, kind, and compassionate, even in heated conversations?
1 — 2 — 3 — 4 — 5 — 6 — 7 — 8 — 9 — 10

5. Are you able to listen to others without being pulled into their feelings, especially when they are discouraged, angry, or sad?

1 — 2 — 3 — 4 — 5 — 6 — 7 — 8 — 9 — 10

6. Can you express your feelings freely and honestly when angry or in a volatile situation?

1 — 2 — 3 — 4 — 5 — 6 — 7 — 8 — 9 — 10

7. Do you feel understood and heard by others?

1 — 2 — 3 — 4 — 5 — 6 — 7 — 8 — 9 — 10

8. When conversations are heated, are you able to listen to others without interrupting or defending yourself?

1 — 2 — 3 — 4 — 5 — 6 — 7 — 8 — 9 — 10

9. Are you comfortable with silence in conversations?

1 — 2 — 3 — 4 — 5 — 6 — 7 — 8 — 9 — 10

10. Are you able to use statements like "I feel" instead of attacking when your intentions or actions are being questioned?

1 — 2 — 3 — 4 — 5 — 6 — 7 — 8 — 9 — 10

If you scored between 76 and 100, congratulations! You have mastered conscious communication practices. Know that your sense of ease and presence during conversations has a healing effect on those who engage with you. You are a model of conscious conversation, and your efforts support others in learning to raise their consciousness when communicating. Continue to honor yourself and those around as you continue your journey towards greater understanding of yourself and those around you.

If you scored between 51 and 75, you are doing a terrific job of developing your conscious communication prowess. The more you are compassionate and comfortable with yourself, the more you will find yourself experiencing the same with others. Focus on the areas in which you scored yourself lower points in this survey and continue the wonderful work that you are already doing!

If you scored between 26 and 50, you have done some work towards conscious communication, but there is room for greater patience and understanding towards yourself and others. Try to stop and catch yourself when you are struggling or feeling defensive. Know that you are not alone and that even by responding to this profile, you are committing yourself to your own personal growth. Your efforts will show. First and foremost, have compassion on yourself and watch it blossom into greater intimacy and connections in your life.

If you scored between 10 and 25, while you have yet to fully develop your conscious communication skills, you have taken the first step. Start by taking small, incremental steps towards more consciousness. For example, for a week, observe the times when you are compelled to interrupt others while conversing. Another week, try to use "I feel" statements when you are feeling under the gun on a conversation. Then be sure to acknowledge yourself for your efforts. Doing so will accelerate your progress and encourage more intimacy in your communications.

Communication is key to success in life. Conscious, heart-centered communication can turn a sour situation into a win-win for all. Unconscious communication, on the other hand, can turn a potentially sweet situation into a raging disaster. The rule is to speak as you would like to be spoken to and listen as you would want to be heard.

Neutralizing Negativity Trigger Situation

Things were getting tense at the office. There were rumors that higher management was laying off staff. The staff were all working their tails off, with a sense that if they slowed down, they would be the first slab of beef on the cutting block. One morning Ruth was informed by a couple of colleagues that a fellow staff member, Joan, was bad-mouthing her to their new manager. Ruth was horrified. She had been working with Joan for a long time, and they had been through a lot together. She felt hurt and betrayed.

The Ego's Response

Kate tells Ruth that Joan has been undermining her with the new boss.

Ruth (immediately reacting to Kate's input): How dare she do that to me! I've actually been complimenting her work and talking her up to management. I can't believe she'd do this, especially since she claims to be my friend. I'm gonna give her a piece of my mind! (Ruth heads over to Joan's desk, feeling angry and reactive.) Joan, Kate just told me that you bad-mouthed me to the boss. What the hell? You are so two-faced.

Joan (also reactive and defensive): I don't know what you are talking about. What did Kate say?

Ruth: She said that you told Sam that I was not holding my weight and that my work was shoddy.

Joan: Well, he asked. All I did was tell him the truth.

Ruth: The truth? You have no idea what I do. And why would he ask? You know, I am constantly supporting you and talking you up to management. No more! And all this time I thought you were my friend. From now on I'm gonna fight fire with fire. Just you wait, girlfriend!

Joan: Go ahead. You don't scare me. Besides, I've beaten you to the punch.

Thereafter there would be a heavy, strained, and toxic environment throughout the department, especially between Joan and Ruth. Kate would also feel betrayed by Ruth, who had mentioned her in her conversation with Joan. Others would have heard the conversation and felt uneasy. The energy of the entire department would be affected. Like begets like. There would be further gossip and toxicity. There would be two warring factions, each trying to pull allies in from other staff members. Vying for the manager's approval, Joan and Ruth would be one-upping each other at staff meetings. Whether they were aware of it or not, the entire department would be energetically drained in response to the toxicity of the situation.

The Heart's Response

Kate tells Ruth about what Joan said. At first Ruth has an impulse to walk over to Joan and attack her lack of integrity, along with defending herself. However, she chooses to refrain and sleep on it.

The next morning, a little calmer, Ruth approaches Joan. She has spent the evening strategizing on how she will breach the subject and how she will conduct herself during the conversation.

Ruth: Good morning, Joan.

Joan: Good morning.

Ruth: Do you have a couple of minutes to chat?

Joan: Only a couple.

Ruth: This won't take long. If it's OK with you, I'd like to talk in private. Can we go out to the stairwell?

Joan: OK.

Ruth (once they are in the stairwell): Joan, I have a concern to discuss, but first, I want you to know that I appreciate and respect you. I think you are terrific at what you do, and while I can't speak for you, I think that the feelings are mutual. Before we begin, I have a couple of requests. I'd appreciate it if we could each take turns speaking, committing to listening attentively to one another and making every effort not to interrupt the other person while speaking. I want you to know that I am committed to working through this situation, so that we both feel a sense of resolve. Is that OK with you?

Joan: Sure.

Ruth: I heard that you criticized my work to our new manager, Sam. I know we've been through a lot together. And I want to say that for my part in this, whatever it may be, I apologize. When I heard that you were criticizing me, I felt hurt and confused. Help me to understand. Is there something I did or said that instigated this? (Ruth was careful not to attack Joan, and was committed to being nonreactive. Her intention was to keep her heart open and to be present.)

Joan: Well, to tell you the truth, I heard that they would be laying someone off, and I'm afraid that it could be me. My husband is not working right now, and I am over sixty years of age. I can't afford to lose my job.

Ruth: Joan, you are a rock star! There's no way that Sam is going to lay you off! I don't think you've got anything to worry about. (Joan doesn't know, and Ruth hasn't told her, that on a couple of occasions Ruth had gone to management and told Sam what an awesome job Joan was doing.)

While Ruth left the conversation without an apology from Joan, she felt a sense of resolution. She did not go back to Sam to redeem herself, nor did she share their discussion with Kate or any other coworkers. In fact, she left the conversation feeling compassion for Joan. Her anger melted into a greater understanding of Joan's situation and why she did what she did.

To recount, here are the strategic steps that Ruth took:

1. She spoke with Joan alone and out of ear range of anyone.
2. She started by sharing her intention to work the situation out.
3. She committed to parameters in which she and Joan would take turns sharing perspectives without interruption from the other.
4. She told Joan that she respected her and the work she did, and that she thought the feelings were mutual.

5. She started her sharing with "I felt." She searched beyond her initial anger and got in touch with the hurt she felt before meeting with Joan. She then honestly shared her feelings and stayed away from verbally attacking her.

6. She actively listened without interrupting Joan.

7. She encouraged Joan and worked towards quelling her concerns.

8. She did not approach the manager afterwards to defend herself. Doing so would have perpetuated the toxicity of the situation. She trusted that her work would speak for itself.

The Witness-self's Response

Kate tells Ruth about what Joan said. Ruth knows that something greater is at play. While she does not ignore Joan's choice, she sees that she energetically plays a role in everything that occurs in her life. She knows that she attracts what she focuses on, and she is not a victim. She surrenders to the experience, without the need to react or respond. The ultimate worst-case outcome is that she is fired. If this happens, she has absolute faith that there are other vocations in store for her and that all will happen as it should. She trusts in this and looks forward to witnessing the next chapter of her life as it unfolds.

Tenets of Mindful Conflict Resolution

• Insist on privacy when having potentially volatile conversations.

- Set into your intentions the question, "How may I serve?"
- Start the conversation with the intention of resolution.
- Set parameters of the conversation before starting:
  1. An intention for resolution.
  2. We both have mutual respect for one another.
  3. We will each take turns speaking.
  4. When one speaks, the other focuses completely on them.
  5. No interruptions are permitted.
- Speak using open-ended questions.
- Avoid sarcasm and innuendo.
- Give the other the benefit of the doubt.
- Ask rather than tell.
- Remain calm and avoid being reactive.
- When necessary, repeat what you have heard to ensure accuracy.
- Take turns speaking, both committing to fully listening to the other, as opposed to building one's own case while the other is speaking.
- When you feel fired up, ask yourself, "Do I want to be right, or do I want to choose love?"
- To stay connected, look into the eyes of the other (especially the left eye).
- Avoid shaming the other person.
- Work from a place of compassion. How would you respond if the other were a child?
- Think before you speak.

Befriending a Person You Abhor

In several instances, I have found that individuals who at first annoyed me could often be transformed into colleagues whom I deeply admire and appreciate.

There was one such woman at a particular job. She immediately turned me off. While I couldn't place it specifically, there was something about her that I did not like.

When I started to look within, I discovered that I was jealous of her. She was highly skilled, creative, and charismatic. She was everything that I wanted to be (and, in my insecure self, believed that I was not). Once I realized this, I worked on changing my mind about her. At first I felt manipulative in our conversations. I would find something complimentary to say or would initiate some idle chitchat. In time, we built a strong friendship, and I was grateful that I was able to move past my jealousy.

Next time a colleague annoys you, ask yourself what in particular it is about them that does so. They may possess traits that you have disowned or disavowed in yourself. They may possess traits that you are jealous of, or very simply they just may not be your cup of tea. Whatever the case, reflect on your feelings. They might provide you with unexpected insights.

Toxic Coworkers

At times a staff member may be clearly toxic; no matter how hard you try, you are unable to make the relationship work in your organization. Unfortunately, we live in a world of lawsuits and liabilities. In such cases it is wise to do the following:

- Keep clear and concise records of their behavior. Include dates, times, what was said, and the actions that were taken. If witnesses are present, make note of that as well. Provide the staff member with written notices, and be sure to have them sign them. Provide them with notifications, timelines, and a definite plan to improve their work efforts, making sure that they sign all notices and documents.

- Listen to staff members, keeping abreast of the workplace from their perspective. They often can provide an early warning of toxicity.

- Do not fire an employee until you have enough documentation to support your action. You want to ensure that you have enough evidence of their toxic behavior.

- Ensure that the employee leaves the workplace immediately upon dismissal. A toxic exit drama would not be good for anyone.

Listen and Love

The more I committed to inner integrity and explored my neediness, the more I realized that I lacked active listening skills. Soon after I realized this, I received a wonderful gift. I became interested in producing when I was responsible for writing the audio book study guides. I attended the recording sessions to write the books, and in doing so, I discovered that I wanted to be a producer.

I approached the vice president and he told me that while he appreciated my interest, I was effective in my current position, and that was where he would like me to remain.

What happened next was remarkable. Within a couple of weeks, he called me back into his office and told me that there had been a change of plans and that they would like me to produce. I was overjoyed.

This was one of many synchronicities that I experienced as I became committed to becoming more intentional and mindful. Each time they occur, I am filled with delight and appreciation. They are gifts that feel so right and so miraculous. They touch the depth of my soul.

In the recording sessions, I noticed how different it was for the authors to be alone in a sound booth compared to speaking to thousands of conference attendees. I noted that the recording process could be extremely tiring, as they had to be highly focused and did not have the energetic exchange with an audience that would support them. So as a producer, I did the unthinkable. I sat in the recording booth with them.

At first the recording engineers were horrified: "You can't go in there. You'll make noise. You have to be absolutely still and not make a move or utter a word while the author is speaking."

Despite the engineers' trepidations, I joined the authors in the booth. I knew that I could energetically support them and be their responsive audience. I could also ask questions of them as they arose. In doing so, their recording would be much more conversational and engaging.

Thus my training in active learning began. I gave 100 percent of my attention to the speaker. If I started to look away to view the outline and find the next question in the queue, the author would feel it. It would distract them and impede the flow of the conversation. I learned to be present and trust that the perfect questions would arise when needed.

So in whatever way you can, I encourage you to practice active listening. While it can be very difficult to begin with, ultimately people will feel heard and understood in your presence. The deeper connections you make will prove to be invaluable.

Building Respectful Communication Parameters

I have belonged to the Shematrix women's support group for several years. At first I found it intimidating, because there were very strict parameters around how we communicated with one another. Once I fully understood them, I was convinced that using those parameters in all conversations would enhance my relationships and build much stronger trust.

Here are the key parameters that I attempt to adhere to in all of my interactions:

- Maintain eye contact when conversing. We often look away when ashamed, embarrassed, or speaking about a difficult topic. Eye contact supports deeper connection.

- When referring to an experience, use "I" instead of "somebody" or "people." When broaching a difficult topic, we often use third-person references. For example, instead of saying, "You know how people get angry when they are interrupted in a conversation?" you say, "I get angry when someone interrupts me during a conversation." Own your discomfort. Speaking from the "I" perspective feels more vulnerable, but ultimately creates greater intimacy and connection.

- When you refer to something someone else said to you, ask their permission before repeating it. For example, Suzy might have said, "I got really angry when my coworker John was patronizing me." Instead of repeating what Suzy said, you ask her permission first: "Suzy, may I refer to what you've just shared?" This invites Suzy to say no if she doesn't want her comment to be repeated. This commitment to integrity in conversation builds greater trust, as it curbs gossip and inaccurate hearsay. We often cite what others say because we feel insecure. Others can serve as scapegoats as opposed to owning our own feelings.

- Do not analyze another's situation. Simply be present and available to listen. Although this can be difficult, jumping into the role of caregiver can be an easy way to avoid dealing with your own feelings and problems. Often people do not have the know-how to advise others: they do more damage than good. To sit and simply witness another's pain often does more for them that trying to fix them.

Another point: when we are uncomfortable with another's tears, we may pat their back, encouraging them not to cry, or we hand them a tissue. These gestures are a distraction that reflects our own discomfort with the feelings being shared. Try to avoid doing so. Don't tell them not to cry—this can be a shaming imposition. Sit in your discomfort and have the faith that by being present and actively listening, you are supporting them.

Shifting Negative Statements to Positive "Thank-You" Statements

I don't believe that you should refrain from apologizing when you have made an error. In fact, it shows greater courage to own your choices and show compassion for the other person. However, because the word "sorry" connotes sorrow, you might want to replace it with "I apologize." If you want to shift your verbiage into even more positive statements, here are some suggestions:

Negative Statement	Positive "Thank You" Statement
"I'm sorry I'm late."	"Thank you for waiting for me."
"I'm sorry, but I cannot attend."	"Thank you for inviting me."
"I'm sorry that I made a mistake."	"Thank you for pointing out my error."
"I'm sorry for being so long-winded."	"Thank you for being such a thoughtful and attentive listener."
"I'm sorry for being so needy lately."	"Thank you for being there for me."
"I'm sorry that I've been so unresponsive."	"Thank you for being so understanding."
"I'm sorry for shaming you."	"Thank you for being a mirror to my own feelings of shame."
"I'm sorry for being so angry."	"Thank you accepting my outburst and not taking it personally."
"I'm sorry for being emotional."	"Thank you for accepting me."

Effective Social Media Communication

While the majority of trigger situations that I shared have been in the form of one-on-one dialogues, I think it is important to discuss trigger situations in the form of email and social media chains. I don't know how many times I have sent reactive emails that I should not have. The energy I was feeling was toxic and perpetuated a chain of ugly and often misconstrued communications. Usually the relationships found resolution once the two of us spoke in person. Sometimes seeing each other face-to-face is optimal. However, email and other social media are useful forms of communication that we are using more and more. Thus we need to take care when using these media. (When in doubt, I encourage you to pick up the phone or meet for a cup of tea and a chat.)

Emotional Email Trigger Situation

A voiceover actor was involved in a recording that had to be rushed in order to meet deadlines. Costs were high and mistakes were made.

The Ego's Response

Jerry was the actor, Laura was the sound engineer, and Mike was the production company representative that hired Jerry and Laura. After the recording, Mike sent the attached email to Jerry:

> Hi Jerry,
> We had a little problem regarding your recording sessions. Both the recording and the number of hours it took to edit added up to much longer than it should have. Your engineer, Laura, said that you were correcting spelling and editing during the session.

Perhaps this was all too rushed and you didn't have enough time to fully review the prior edits that we had made to the script. In future, we hope that will take the necessary time to review the script so that you can go into the studio better prepared. In the future, we also hope you will practice reading it out loud several times so the recording will go smoothly.

The reprimanding undercurrent of the email, while subtle, connotes a fear-based response to the situation. Engineer Laura's bill was higher than Mike had anticipated, and he was reprimanding Jerry because he was feeling threatened himself. He copied the production company's CEO on his reprimanding email as a means of protecting himself. Prior to the email Mike contacted the engineer, Laura, about her high fees. In turn, Laura felt threatened and proceeded to find ways to justify her editing fees, defending herself and making others (Jerry and the book editors) wrong—further creating a chain of fear-based, accusatory reactivity.

Jerry's response (below) is also fear-based. He is defending himself and his position:

Good morning, Mike. I am upset by your email and do not appreciate the accusatory tone. I'm disappointed that you didn't reach out to me prior to making the assumptions that you did.

I would like to make it clear that I reviewed each and every one of the proofreader's edits. The corrections that I made during the recording were edits that were missed by the proofreader. In all honesty, it was very frustrating for me to have to stop the recordings over seventy times to make editing notes. Perhaps in future someone else could do a final once-over proofread. I agree with you in that I do not want to have to go through that again. But I was in no way at fault in failing to adequately review the script. Having to stop and start during the recording took way too long, and added a great deal more time to Laura's edits. By the time the script reaches the recording studio, it should be performance/reader ready.

Given that your recording request was last-minute, I believe that I pulled it all together with very little forewarning, and should be credited rather than reprimanded. I had to make adjustments in order to fit the recording session into my schedule. For the next recording:

- Have someone do a final proofreading scan before we record. I don't claim to be a proofreader; I am an actor.
- In future I will take the time to read the script aloud prior to recording. However, I want to emphasize that the quality of my reading was not the issue, and I take offense that it was raised as a reason for the slowdown and the additional costs incurred.

By following these suggestions, I believe costs will be substantially lower.

Note how lengthy and time-consuming Jerry's response is. Because *this communication chain is ego-* and fear-based, the relationship has weakened, and it will take some energy, commitment, and time to rebuild it to one of trust and good will.

The Heart's Response

Note the clarity, length, and energy of the two heart-based emails below. The tone of Mike's email to Jerry is not defensive. It is open-hearted and non-reactive:

Hi Jerry,

Thank you for taking on this project at such late notice. We really appreciate your efforts! I wanted to ask you about the recording session. If I'm going to be really honest, I was surprised by Laura's bill and want to see if there is some way that we can lower the bill for future recordings. I got Laura's perspective, and I wanted to get yours as well.

Laura mentioned that you spent quite some time correcting grammar errors during the session. Is there a way that this might be rectified next time around?

I look forward to hearing your perspective. We want to make these recordings a win-win for all!

The tone of this heart-based email is inquisitive and supportive. Feeling supported, Jerry's response is also heart-based. He is not feeling defensive, and his position is proactive as opposed to reactive:

Good morning, Mike. Thanks for checking in. The recording session was a challenge because of the time spent making textual corrections on the spot. It really slowed down the process, affected the flow, and created a great deal more editing challenges for Laura. While I thought the proofreader's edits were terrific, there were several typos and edits I found during the recording session. For future recordings, I have three suggestions:

- Perhaps a third eye to proof would help so that the script is reader-ready for the recording session. (I know someone who is extremely reasonable. Please let me know if you'd like to get her involved.)

- While I don't usually do so, I would be happy to do a read-through aloud prior to the session to further catch any missed edits.

- As far as Laura's bill is concerned, I'm sorry that it was higher than you anticipated. From her perspective, it is always difficult to estimate the anticipated hours, and the stops and starts for editing corrections really added to the editing time involved.

In all honesty, having to make the edits really slowed down the recording and affected the flow. I think that in future with an additional eye to scan the manuscript, we will not have issues. All the best and thanks for you supportive email! I too look forward to great success with the project.

Again, note the length of the emails when the conversation is heart-based. There is much more clarity and flow because the writers' minds were not cluttered with fear or defensive thinking. The communication was proactive and supportive and reflects a higher consciousness. The relationship among all parties continues to flourish.

The Witness-self's Response

This email communication would be similar to the heart-based communique, but there would be an element of complete ease, trust, and compassion energetically underlying the situation. There would be an element of both faith and gratitude, as opposed to the tension and anxiety displayed in the fear-based communication.

Tips for Conscious Communication in Email and Social Media

- If you feel triggered and reactive, abstain from responding. Ideally wait until you are able to respond from a heart-centered place.

- When responding, you may find it difficult to go directly to your heart. If you want to try, put your hands on your heart and take some deep breaths. Imagine your heart filling with compassionate, healing, white light. See that light starting at the core of your heart and radiating outwards. See the light filling every cell of your body, every thought and emotion. Then if possible, see the light permeating the person with whom you are triggered (often this may not be possible, and that's OK). Say "yes" to healing the experience, and ask that the highest good of all be served in the situation. Set an intention to heal the situation and to respond from an open heart and mind. Ask Source or your highest self if there is anything you need to hear before responding. Then if and when you feel ready, respond.

- Avoid using accusatory language. Go to your feelings and use "I" statements. For example, instead of using phrases like, "When you said X, you made me feel Y," use phrases like, "I felt sad when . . ." or "I was disappointed when . . ." or "After reading your email, I felt . . ."

- Avoid third-party references. For example, "Our friend M said that you have been talking about me behind my back." Stay with the person you are engaging with. Bringing others into the scenario will escalate the toxicity, muddy the waters, and create more chaos and fear.

- Read your email response aloud before sending it. Doing so will provide you with greater insight into the energy that you are transmitting.

- I can't emphasize enough how important it is, if your email is inflammatory, to sit on it for a while until you have calmed down. Don't forget: it is a record of the exchange that cannot be erased. It cannot be undone.

- With a social media chain that triggers you, these same suggestions apply. Before responding, you may want to ask yourself:

   Is publicly expressing your opinion worth your energy?

   Will your response elevate the conversation or add to a fear-based, ego-driven exchange?

   Why do you feel the need to engage in the conversation? Go into any upset you feel as you read the trigger piece, and get clear about what upsets you. Instead of lashing out, look for the healing opportunity.

   Is your contribution fear-based or love-based? If it is fear-based, will it truly be of service? What might happen if, instead of responding, you sit with the judgment that wells up inside of you? Might it be a healing opportunity?

   Will your perspective help other onlookers to heal, or will it further perpetuate a negative communication chain?

Is your criticism perpetuating a cycle of prejudice and black-and-white thinking? Are you judging their judgments and hating their hatred? If so, might your time be better spent sending light to yourself and the other?

Owning your part in "dis-eased" communication is not simple, but it is a necessary step in your evolution. Imagine if world leaders and key business decision makers took more time being reflective and introspective and less time being reactive. If we all made raising our consciousness a priority over anything else, what a magical world this would be!

Habit 9

THANK All Support Channels

*Authentic and heartfelt gratitude is a grace that shifts
the energy of a business to the core. Being grateful
exponentially produces more and more to be grateful
for. Manage, model, and move from a place of
deepest gratitude, and success is yours.*

Experiencing gratitude can be the most surefire way
to effect the greatest transformations in your life.
Once you shift your mindset from what you don't have
to what you have and are grateful for, the outer world
begins to reflect your uplifted inner state. Integrating
an attitude of gratitude into all you do will shift not
only your mindset but the environment in which you
work as well. Once you begin to invoke the 3 T's—
trust, transformation, and *treasure*—you will note a
massive shift.

If you suffer from a "lack" mindset, it can be very
difficult to pull yourself out of it. However, when
you focus on what you don't have, every part of you

responds to that sense of lack, including your subconscious. If you energetically resonate to a consciousness of lack, you will magnetically draw more of the same into your life. What you focus on becomes your reality. Shifting from what you lack to what you have in the workplace is one of the most transformative Good Morning steps you can take towards greater success.

Gratitude Profile

Before you delve deeper into Habit 9, it is helpful to get a sense of just how grateful you are for the life that you lead. For each of the questions below, choose the number that most closely aligns with your current situation (1 being "not at all" and 10 being "a great deal").

1. Do you spend most of your day feeling grateful for your life?

1 — 2 — 3 — 4 — 5 — 6 — 7 — 8 — 9 — 10

2. Are you excited even by the little gifts that come your way?

1 — 2 — 3 — 4 — 5 — 6 — 7 — 8 — 9 — 10

3. Do you feel joy about your friendships?

1 — 2 — 3 — 4 — 5 — 6 — 7 — 8 — 9 — 10

4. Do you often thank your Creator for your wonderful life?

1 — 2 — 3 — 4 — 5 — 6 — 7 — 8 — 9 — 10

5. Are you in awe of nature and its splendor?

1 — 2 — 3 — 4 — 5 — 6 — 7 — 8 — 9 — 10

6. Do you often experience gratitude to the point of tears?

1 — 2 — 3 — 4 — 5 — 6 — 7 — 8 — 9 — 10

7. Do you thank people for the way they affect you?

1 — 2 — 3 — 4 — 5 — 6 — 7 — 8 — 9 — 10

8. Do you express gratitude for the food that you eat?

1 — 2 — 3 — 4 — 5 — 6 — 7 — 8 — 9 — 10

9. Do you often exclaim, "It doesn't get better than this!"?

1 — 2 — 3 — 4 — 5 — 6 — 7 — 8 — 9 — 10

10. Do you get excited about your future, feeling gratitude for what you have already experienced and for what is to come?

1 — 2 — 3 — 4 — 5 — 6 — 7 — 8 — 9 — 10

If you scored between 76 and 100, congratulations! You already experience a great deal of gratitude. Know that it has brought more to be grateful for into your life. Continue to express gratitude to yourself, your creators, and others. As you do so, you will continue to watch miracles abound.

If you scored between 51 and 75, you are doing a terrific job at expressing and experiencing gratitude. The more you focus what you are grateful for, the more you will tap into a life of ease and grace. Where do you feel any struggle with gratitude? Focus on the areas in which you scored yourself lower points in this survey and continue the wonderful work that you are already doing.

If you scored between 26 and 50, you have done some work towards cultivating more gratitude into your life, but there is room for even more. When possible, stop and watch yourself when you see yourself as a victim in your life. Whenever you can, look for the lessons and the silver linings in every situation. Know that it takes commitment to view everything in your life from a place of gratitude. When in doubt, ask your Creator for help.

If you scored between 10 and 25, you have yet to fully develop an attitude of gratitude, but you have taken the first step. Start by taking small, incremental steps towards gratitude. For example, each day focus on one simple thing that you are grateful for in your life. It may be as basic as a food that you enjoyed eating or a song that lifted your spirits.

Whatever your score has been in this profile, you may want to start a gratitude journal. Doing so focuses you further on gratitude and strengthens your commitment to experiencing more of it.

Building Trust
An essential component to building your gratitude muscles is cultivating faith and trusting that the uni-

verse has your back. If you sit in distrust and wait for evidence of change, you will not be successful. Starting your day, and every possible transaction, with a "yes" attitude is the first step towards building that trust in yourself and your colleagues. If you have followed the practices and principles in this book, you will have already cultivated a great deal of trust in your workplace. The more you function with an open heart and the more you are committed to inner integrity, the more others will see you as honesty and trustworthy.

Trust-Building Trigger Situation

The other day Julie made an error at the childcare facility she was working at. She was feeling very sick and shouldn't have been working, but they were short-staffed. Because she was feeling ill, she had much less patience. When a parent came to pick up her child, Julie reprimanded the child for her poor behavior. Her mother demanded an apology. The next day the daycare manager told her that the mother had complained. The manager was surprised, because she knew Julie to be patient and kind with the children.

The Ego's Response

Had Julie responded from a reactive, fear-based stance, she would have told her manager that the mother was overreacting and that she, Julie, did nothing wrong. Julie would have spent a great deal of time trying to defend herself and justify her actions, doing everything she could to look good in the manager's eyes. She would probably not have conversed with the mother but would have made her the "enemy." Each time she came by, Julie would be seething, focusing on how the mother had wronged her. She would find fault with the child and the woman's mothering skills. She would gossip with her fellow teachers, bad-mouthing the child and her mother, trying to elicit stories about the child's misbehavior in order to alleviate her own feelings of inadequacy. She would have built a quagmire of ugliness around the situation that would grow and fester. Ultimately, the negative energy would affect everyone involved and the daycare center.

The Heart's Response

In this case, even though the manager told Julie that speaking with the mother was not necessary, Julie would want to do so. Before doing this, she would take an integrity inventory. She would ask herself: How might I have been wrong? Was I overreactive or insensitive because I was feeling sick? Was I my "best self" in dealing with this situation? What might I have done differently? She would then meet with the mother to discuss the incident. Prior to the meeting, she would be clear in her intention to own her part and heal the situation.

In the meeting, Julie would start by apologizing for her part in the situation. She would give the mother time to vent and share her experience with her, without interrupting. After the mother felt complete in her response, Julie would restate her apology, making no excuses. Very often when we are willing to let our guard down and simply apologize, the other person can be taken aback by the apology. They rarely anticipate a fullhearted apology, nor do they expect the other party to take responsibility. Cultivating trust can lead to gratitude for the deeper, heart-centered connection that is nurtured. In this case, Julie would have learned a valuable lesson. The mother would have seen that Julie was willing to take ownership of her errors, and would know that she could depend upon her.

The Witness-self's Response

The witness-self or highest self would not have even gone to the place of finding fault. There would be an acceptance of the situation as a learning tool that allowed both parties to grow from the experience. It would have been viewed as perfect in the scheme of life as it unfolds.

By having a candid conversation with the child's mother, Julie was able to free the tension between them. The mother felt heard, and Julie felt trusted. A couple of weeks after their conversation, the mother came to pick up her child. At the moment she arrived, Julie and her child were in a place of creativity and love as they danced to the song "Let It Go" from the movie *Frozen*. They were both experiencing the joy and connection that comes when one is inspired. Perhaps the mother walking in at that moment was a miracle.

The mother asked how her daughter was doing, and Julie responded that they were both doing wonderfully well. Was owning her part in the exchange worth it? Absolutely. While the mother may have had a stronger reaction because of her own life's challenges, what she was going through was none of Julie's business and had nothing to do with her part in the exchange. Julie's business was to right the wrong that she created.

Gratitude and appreciation are transformative. If you get nothing else from this book, know that shifting your consciousness from focusing on lack to focusing on gratitude will in and of itself transform your life. Appreciating what you have, from the smallest of treasures to the largest, will make you feel enriched and enlivened.

Innovative Implementation Ideas

There are many ways to build a greater attitude of gratitude in the workplace. Here are a few ideas:

- Have a two- to three-minute joy break twice a day, when fun music is played over a loudspeaker and staff are encouraged to shake out their anxieties and dance themselves into a more energized state.

- Conduct weekly success story cheerleading meetings. Here your staff share the stories of their success or the success of their colleagues. If you can create a success shout-out that encourages staff to support their coworkers, a spirit of non-competitiveness and generosity will flourish.

• Have staff commit to a deadline that they themselves set and keep. My friend Larry New offered this powerful suggestion: Each employee is different. As a manager, you have to learn who they are as individuals and what works best for them. Having employees set their own deadlines is empowering and shows respect for them. A good manager should also be willing to train their staff out of their current position. Doing so prioritizes them and their work over the status quo. Empowering staff in this way creates gratitude in them for the space that you provide and for your trust in them.

• Have a refresh room in the business, where staff can have a power nap, meditate, or decompress. Provide calming music (432 hertz is very relaxing), a small fountain, sand, doodle art, an alarm clock, pillows, and a warm blanket—anything that helps them feel relaxed.

• Have an annual "Just Because You Are You" celebration honoring your staff for their efforts. You could offer dinner (or a potluck if finances are a challenge) and acknowledge each contributor for their efforts.

- Integrate "joy" practices into your daily routine
  and watch your productivity soar. Involve as
  many staff as possible in brainstorming sessions.
  In these meetings, applaud audacity and encourage out-of-the-box thinking. Let your staff know
  that there are no bad ideas, and that often the best
  results start as apparently insane seedlings. Create an atmosphere that encourages creativity.

- Have a daily meditation break when staff are
  encouraged to quiet their minds and cultivate
  mindfulness. It would be ideal if a staff member
  could lead the session, although there are videos
  and audios that could serve the same purpose.
  Make the meditation a place of nonjudgment.
  Ideally the break could last up to thirty minutes,
  but if some people quit after five minutes, so be it.
  Not to worry—what you lose in "productive work
  time" you gain in a calmer, more engaged, and
  energized staff. You could begin or end the session
  with a gratitude inventory in which participants
  are asked to visualize all that they are grateful for
  in their lives.

- Have a gratitude box at the office. Each day before
  leaving, every staff member puts a piece of paper
  listing one event or experience that they were
  grateful for that day. At the end of every month,
  pull out one piece of paper, and the winner gets a
  free lunch or a small gift.

- Plan monthly staff events outside of the workplace that encourage camaraderie and joyful play. You could go to an amusement arcade, racetrack, or harbor boat tour. You could also engage in bowling, ice skating, or any other event that encourages childlike fun.

When you create an environment when staff feel appreciated, cared for, and honored, they will naturally want to contribute and will find a great deal of satisfaction in the work they do. You will have much less turnover when you focus on how you can best serve your staff so that they can best serve your clientele.

Sharing Breeds Caring

A friend of mine involved in industrial engineering once shared with me some insights of one of the more successful Japanese corporate models. He said that they create a system in which the employees share in ownership of the business. When the business thrives, they do as well. They are incentivized to do their best. For this reason, turnover is low and productivity is maximized. It creates a win-win scenario for all involved.

Whenever you have an opportunity to share your successes with your staff, don't hesitate to do so. If they feel they are vital and appreciated contributors to the business, they are more apt to remain with you for the long haul.

A Final Note on Causeless Joy

Earlier in the book I mentioned causeless joy. What is causeless joy? It could be defined as joy, just because; joy without any particular cause. I have recently experienced this phenomenon myself. It happens most often when I am practicing mindfulness meditation. I end my sessions focusing on what I am most grateful for. Often I feel a tickle at the center of my being. Then before I know it, just like the meditators at the temple in India, I am cackling away. Tears of laughter and release fall from my eyes, and I giggle from the center of my heart. As I say a resounding "yes" to my life, my heart grows more and more open. Wherever I go, be it at work or at play, my joyful heart follows. As I commit to inner integrity, I grow closer to fully loving who I am. I am starting to recognize that there is much more to me than the body I inhabit, the mind that catches the thoughts that pass through it, and the emotions that sometime cloud this personality-self.

While I can't promise you causeless joy, I suggest that you set the intention to experience it. Make joy and laughter the center of your desires, and choose to live and love your best self. When you do, you will experience a connection and freedom that is unlike anything you have ever experienced before.

Gratitude Visualization

As a final exercise, practice this gratitude visualization whenever you feel your energy or hope depleting.

Note how you feel prior to doing it, and then note again how you feel afterwards. You will note quite an energy shift.

Find a quiet spot where you can sit undisturbed for at least five minutes. Make yourself comfortable, sitting in a chair with your spine erect. Take several breaths in, holding them for three seconds, and then exhaling. With each inhalation, see fresh, cool air entering your nostrils. With each exhalation, imagine all of your bodily and emotional tensions melting away.

Then gradually scan your life, starting at birth and moving forward. Allow wonderful memories of delight to flood into your mind's eye. As each joyful memory appears, say a resounding, "Yes. Thank you!" Allow your heart to fully express the gratitude as it arises. If other thoughts arise, be thankful for those as well. Whatever appears in your mind's eye, respond with a "Yes. Thank you!" Once you reach the present day, allow your mind's eye to project into the future. Experience all of the hopes and dreams that you have deposited into your emotional wish box as if they are happening in the present, and again, to each image, respond, "Yes. Thank you!" Continue doing this until the images subside and you are left with a joyful "yes" smile on your face. Open your eyes and if inspired, physicalize your gratitude. Dance, sing, draw, cook, write or find other creative ways of expressing it. Doing so further raises your energy (this is often when I experience causeless joy).

Move forward with your day, knowing that the work to manifest your joys has already been done. The day is yours and the moment is now!

I hope that the habits I have outlined in this book can support a greater sense of peace, integrity, and mindfulness in your workplace. Know that by reading it, you have already taken massive action, having opened a portal to deeper love and understanding that cannot be taken away. Your life will change, for you are now the wiser.

References

American Psychiatric Association. *Diagnostic and Statistical Manual of Mental Disorders*. Fifth edition. Arlington, Va.: American Psychiatric Association, 2013.

Cavaiola, Alan A., and Neil J. Lavender. *Toxic Workers: How to Deal with Dysfunctional People on the Job*. Oakland, Calif.: New Harbinger, 2000.

Durvasula, Romani, and Kyle Kittleson, "Ever Felt Fear of Humiliation? Avoidant Personality Disorder May Be Why." MedCircle series, YouTube, May 7, 2019.

Hyacinth, Brigette. "Leadership Is an Action, Not a Position!" LinkedIn, June 18, 2019.

Tolle, Eckhart. "What Is the Purpose of Mental Illness?" www.eckharttollenow.com, 2013.

About the Author

Theresa Puskar is a highly skilled transformation leader, inspirational communicator and author. She has written over 50 motivational books and study guides, she has also authored seven children's books and a critically acclaimed solo stage production, *Causeless Joy*. The founder of *Edu-Tainment Productions*, she is an outstanding and versatile entertainer, weaving profound and often hilarious storytelling into all that she does. Known for her authenticity and unique ability to stir the hearts and minds of those with whom she engages, her refreshing and heartfelt *"tell it like it is"* approach to edu-taining supports greater compassion, consciousness and joy among her audiences.

CPSIA information can be obtained
at www.ICGtesting.com
Printed in the USA
JSHW020244190520
5762JS00005B/13

9 781722 502676